D0907384

Scratch 2.0 Beginner's Guide
Second Edition

Create digital stories, games, art, and animations through six unique projects

Michael Badger

BIRMINGHAM - MUMBAI

Scratch 2.0 Beginner's Guide
Second Edition

Copyright © 2014 Packt Publishing

All rights reserved. No part of this book may be reproduced, stored in a retrieval system, or transmitted in any form or by any means, without the prior written permission of the publisher, except in the case of brief quotations embedded in critical articles or reviews.

Every effort has been made in the preparation of this book to ensure the accuracy of the information presented. However, the information contained in this book is sold without warranty, either express or implied. Neither the author, nor Packt Publishing, and its dealers and distributors will be held liable for any damages caused or alleged to be caused directly or indirectly by this book.

Packt Publishing has endeavored to provide trademark information about all of the companies and products mentioned in this book by the appropriate use of capitals. However, Packt Publishing cannot guarantee the accuracy of this information.

First Published: July 2009

Second Edition: April 2014

Production Reference: 1080414

Published by Packt Publishing Ltd.
Livery Place
35 Livery Street
Birmingham B3 2PB, UK.

ISBN 978-1-78216-072-4

www.packtpub.com

Cover Image by Ross Manges (ross@rossmanges.net)

Credits

Author

Michael Badger

Reviewers

Samyak Bhuta

Manuel Menezes de Sequeira

Franklin Webber

Acquisition Editor

Joanne Fitzpatrick

Content Development Editor

Dayan Hyames

Technical Editors

Shubhangi Dhamgaye

Shweta Pant

Mrunmayee Patil

Aman Preet Singh

Copy Editors

Sarang Chari

Brandt D'Mello

Mradula Hegde

Project Coordinator

Binny K. Babu

Proofreaders

Simran Bhogal

Maria Gould

Ameesha Green

Paul Hindle

Indexer

Mehreen Deshmukh

Production Coordinator

Nitesh Thakur

Cover Work

Nitesh Thakur

About the Author

Michael Badger is a writer and technical communicator who has worked in a range of technical roles, including support, automated software testing, and project management. He has authored several books for Packt Publishing, including *Scratch 1.4 Beginner's Guide*. He also authors a regular Scratch column for Raspberry Pi Geek Magazine, which focuses on Scratch 1.4.

I'd like to thank the team at Packt Publishing for putting up with me and helping me make this revision the best it could be. My loving wife Christie and son Cameron also deserve credit for allowing me the flexibility to complete this book.

About the Reviewers

Samyak Bhuta is fascinated by art and technology and is always excited when they both meet. He is a software architect by profession with over a decade of experience. He started programming in his childhood with GWBasic and quickly moved over to QBasic. Professionally, he has worked on Java, JavaScript, Python, and PHP. He enjoys coding user interfaces as well as working on backend programming. Samyak believes in the open source philosophy and has been active in his local community. He loves to eat dal bati, an Indian dish, and has dreams to become a flautist.

> I would like to thank Packt Publishing for keeping patience when I couldn't submit my reviews on time.

Manuel Menezes de Sequeira has been teaching programming since 1995. He started teaching programming using C, then moved to C++, and later to Java. Nowadays, in his lectures, he usually starts programming with Scratch and Snap!, and then moves on to text-based languages such as Java. Manuel teaches at the Universidade Europeia | Laureate International Universities in Lisbon, Portugal, where he also champions in CoderDojo LX, the Lisbon-based CoderDojo, where children can learn to program for free while having fun. He lives in Lisbon, Portugal, and has been involved for a few years in the translation of Scratch, SNAP!, and other projects to Portuguese.

Franklin Webber is a software professional whose professional experience comes from a testing background where he sought to automate himself out of a job. A college teaching assistant once told Frank that he was a great software developer and a terrible computer scientist, and that the software he wrote cared more for the user experience than the size of its Big O Notation. As a software developer, he became the resident generalist who was always willing to step up to learn new technologies. He now spends most of his time teaching software design to students, both young and old.

www.PacktPub.com

Support files, eBooks, discount offers, and more

You might want to visit www.PacktPub.com for support files and downloads related to your book.

Did you know that Packt offers eBook versions of every book published, with PDF and ePub files available? You can upgrade to the eBook version at www.PacktPub.com and as a print book customer, you are entitled to a discount on the eBook copy. Get in touch with us at service@packtpub.com for more details.

At www.PacktPub.com, you can also read a collection of free technical articles, sign up for a range of free newsletters and receive exclusive discounts and offers on Packt books and eBooks.

http://PacktLib.PacktPub.com

Do you need instant solutions to your IT questions? PacktLib is Packt's online digital book library. Here, you can access, read and search across Packt's entire library of books.

Why Subscribe?

- Fully searchable across every book published by Packt
- Copy and paste, print and bookmark content
- On demand and accessible via web browser

Free Access for Packt account holders

If you have an account with Packt at www.PacktPub.com, you can use this to access PacktLib today and view nine entirely free books. Simply use your login credentials for immediate access.

Table of Contents

Preface

This book demystifies Scratch programming through a variety of projects. The book assumes that you have no programming experience when you begin reading, but by the time you reach the last page, you will be ready to explore your own projects and help other people with Scratch.

The projects start with simpler concepts and get progressively more complicated in terms of programming concepts and design. You will learn how to make multiple-scene stories, think through the logic of a fast-paced arcade game called *Breakout*, interact with a snarky fortune teller, and more. The book's projects tend to demonstrate a programming concept first and then discuss the concept in more detail.

You will receive a balanced introduction to Scratch and universal programming concepts as you create digital stores, animations, and games. With a firm grasp on the fundamentals, you'll be ready to take on more advanced topics and projects.

What this book covers

Chapter 1, Welcome to Scratch 2.0, introduces Scratch and the various types of projects covered in the book.

Chapter 2, A Quick Start Guide to Scratch, takes us on a tour of the online Scratch community. In this chapter, we will create our first Scratch animation while learning basic programming concepts such as loops.

Chapter 3, Creating an Animated Birthday Card, will guide us through how to use Scratch's built-in paint editor to draw bitmap and vector images. To create the card, we will learn important programming concepts such as project initialization, object naming, and event coordination.

Chapter 4, Creating a Scratch Story Book, will guide us through how to build a joke book and coordinate scene changes as a way to navigate through the book. The chapter introduces sound and coordinates as a way to move sprites.

Chapter 5, Creating a Multimedia Slideshow, will guide us through how to create a personalized slideshow by uploading files from our computer. We will also work on resizing images and recording slide narrations that can be played on demand.

Chapter 6, Making an Arcade Game – Breakout (Part I), remixes the classic Pong game into our own brick-busting version called Breakout. We'll clone sprites, estimate direction, and create custom variables to develop the framework of the game.

Chapter 7, Programming a Challenging Gameplay – Breakout (Part II), builds on our Breakout game from the previous chapter. Here, we make the gameplay more challenging by programming the ball speed and reducing the paddle size based on the gameplay. Important concepts include custom procedures, Boolean values, and cloud data.

Chapter 8, Chatting with a Fortune Teller, deals with our game of fortune, where a fortune teller will provide a random fortune in response to the user's typed question. We will work with lists, track intervals with mod, and split words apart to identify individual words.

Chapter 9, Turning Geometric Patterns into Art Using the Pen Tool, combines all the programming concepts we've learned so far to draw art using simple math equations, polygons, and string art. The projects will show you how to take user-defined values and turn them into shapes. This chapter also explains how to apply color and shades to Scratch projects.

Appendix A, Connecting a PicoBoard to Scratch 1.4, emphasizes on projects that use a computer's webcam and the PicoBoard, which is an add-on device capable of running on Scratch 1.4 on the Raspberry Pi. The PicoBoard project incorporates an experiment that measures the resistance of warming water using a thermistor and generates graphs for it.

What you need for this book

To create projects using the Scratch 2 project editor, you need a relatively recent web browser (Chrome 7 or later, Firefox 4 or later, or Internet Explorer 7 or later) with Adobe Flash Player Version 10.2 or later installed. Scratch 2 is designed to support a screen resolution of 1024 x 768 or larger. If your computer doesn't meet these requirements, you can try downloading and installing Scratch 1.4, which you can still use to share projects to the Scratch 2 website.

An offline Scratch 2 editor is also available. You can also still use Scratch 1.4. Note that you can have both Scratch 1.4 and 2 on your computer.

The software to download are as follows:

- The Scratch 2 offline editor can be downloaded from the following link:
  `http://scratch.mit.edu/scratch2download`

- The Scratch 1.4 editor can be downloaded from the following link:
  `http://scratch.mit.edu/scratch_1.4`

Who this book is for

The author approaches the content in this book with the belief that we are all teachers and that you are reading this book not only because you want to learn, but also because you want to share your knowledge with others. Motivated students can pick up this book and teach themselves how to program because the book takes a simple, strategic, and structured approach to learning Scratch.

Parents can grasp the fundamentals so that they can guide their children through introductory Scratch programming exercises. It's therefore perfect for homeschool families. Teachers of all disciplines from Computer Science to English can also quickly get up to speed with Scratch and adapt the projects for use in the classroom.

Conventions

In this book, you will find several headings that appear frequently.

To give clear instructions of how to complete a procedure or task, we use:

Time for action – heading

1. Action 1
2. Action 2
3. Action 3

Instructions often need some extra explanation so that they make sense, so they are followed with:

What just happened?

This heading explains the working of tasks or instructions that you have just completed.

You will also find some other learning aids in the book, including:

Pop quiz – heading

These are short multiple-choice questions intended to help you test your own understanding.

Have a go hero – heading

These practical challenges give you ideas for experimenting with what you have learned.

You will also find a number of styles of text that distinguish between different kinds of information. Here are some examples of these styles, and an explanation of their meaning.

Code words in text, database table names, folder names, filenames, file extensions, pathnames, dummy URLs, user input, and Twitter handles are shown as follows: "Conditional statements are used to check whether a statement is `true` or `false`. For example, `if 4 > 0` is a conditional statement."

New terms and **important words** are shown in bold. Words that you see on the screen, in menus or dialog boxes for example, appear in the text like this: "The top of the page contains the **Create**, **Explore**, and **Discuss** links."

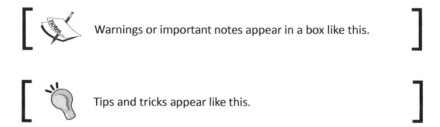

Warnings or important notes appear in a box like this.

Tips and tricks appear like this.

Reader feedback

Feedback from our readers is always welcome. Let us know what you think about this book—what you liked or may have disliked. Reader feedback is important for us to develop titles that you really get the most out of.

To send us general feedback, simply send an e-mail to `feedback@packtpub.com`, and mention the book title through the subject of your message.

If there is a topic that you have expertise in and you are interested in either writing or contributing to a book, see our author guide on `www.packtpub.com/authors`.

Customer support

Now that you are the proud owner of a Packt book, we have a number of things to help you to get the most from your purchase.

Downloading the example code

You can download the example code files for all Packt books you have purchased from your account at http://www.packtpub.com. If you purchased this book elsewhere, you can visit http://www.packtpub.com/support and register to have the files e-mailed directly to you.

Downloading the color images of this book

We also provide you a PDF file that has color images of the screenshots/diagrams used in this book. The color images will help you better understand the changes in the output. You can download this file from: https://www.packtpub.com/sites/default/files/downloads/0724OT_coloredimages.pdf.

Errata

Although we have taken every care to ensure the accuracy of our content, mistakes do happen. If you find a mistake in one of our books—maybe a mistake in the text or the code—we would be grateful if you would report this to us. By doing so, you can save other readers from frustration and help us improve subsequent versions of this book. If you find any errata, please report them by visiting http://www.packtpub.com/submit-errata, selecting your book, clicking on the **errata submission form** link, and entering the details of your errata. Once your errata are verified, your submission will be accepted and the errata will be uploaded to our website, or added to any list of existing errata, under the Errata section of that title.

Piracy

Piracy of copyright material on the Internet is an ongoing problem across all media. At Packt, we take the protection of our copyright and licenses very seriously. If you come across any illegal copies of our works, in any form, on the Internet, please provide us with the location address or website name immediately so that we can pursue a remedy.

Please contact us at copyright@packtpub.com with a link to the suspected pirated material.

We appreciate your help in protecting our authors, and our ability to bring you valuable content.

Questions

You can contact us at questions@packtpub.com if you are having a problem with any aspect of the book, and we will do our best to address it.

1
Welcome to Scratch 2.0

I assume you're reading this book because you want to learn how to create interactive stories, animations, and games using Scratch, or you want to learn Scratch so that you can teach someone else how to program. It matters not whether your classroom is in a middle school, a home school environment, an after-school workshop, or a weekend coding project with your son or daughter. We are all teachers. That's the perspective of this book. You'll learn how to create projects using Scratch so that you can teach someone else, but no programming knowledge is expected.

In this chapter, we will:

- Review what Scratch is and how we can use it
- Learn more about the types of projects we will create in this book
- Explore an example project from the Scratch website and review the project editor

Whether you're 8 or 80, the Scratch programming language provides a beginner-friendly computer programming environment that enables you to create digital projects. Success with Scratch comes quickly. You won't find any quirky syntax to learn, and you won't make any typing mistakes that prevent your program from running.

Creating a project in Scratch is as easy as snapping the color-coded blocks together. This environment allows us to see the positive results quickly. In addition to this, Scratch helps turn passive users into creators.

You'll find comfort in Scratch's building-block approach to create animations, games, and stories. After using Scratch, programming will make sense. It will seem easy. It will bring a smile to your face, and you'll be able to cope with technical concepts in the future.

About Scratch

Mitch Resnick and the Lifelong Kindergarten Group at the Massachusetts Institute of Technology (MIT) in the Media Laboratory developed Scratch as a teaching language primarily for 8 – 16 year olds, but there's nothing stopping the rest of us from enjoying the Scratch experience and sharpening our creative minds.

Encouraging everyone to think programmatically

The natural reaction of people is to see Scratch as a means of teaching computer science and integrating it into classrooms of all levels. There are teachers who use Scratch across a variety of subjects as seen on the ScratchEd site. The ScratchEd site caters to the educational community and aggregates a lot of Scratch resources, including lesson plans and tips. However, the approach and thoroughness of the included material varies greatly. You can check out ScratchEd at `http://scratched.media.mit.edu/`.

While writing this book, I did not set out to write a computer science textbook. It's quite simply a tutorial for people who want to learn how to use Scratch to create stories, animations, games, or art. It primarily addresses the parents, home school families, and teachers who may not be programmers themselves but want a fun way to help their children become more digitally literate. Everyone, however, can use this tutorial to learn Scratch, and many young students have worked through the Version 1.4 of Scratch of this book. I expect young scratchers will be more than capable of working through the projects in this edition.

My underlying belief is that knowing how to program can benefit everyone, but not everyone needs to be a programmer. The mental work required to create a program inherently develops an understanding of how computers work, sharpens our critical thinking skills, and gives us lots of practice at solving problems.

There's also an increasingly popular idea that sometimes we want to create applications for personal use. Of course, system administrators have always created custom scripts to help automate repetitive tasks. However, modern applications such as Scratch or the **MIT App Inventor** (originally developed by Google) make it incredibly easy to create programs for personal use or with the intention of sharing it with a small group of friends, which counters the perspective that learning to program is synonymous with wanting to be a professional programmer or an application developer.

When you have a little bit of programming knowledge, you'll approach non-programming problems in a different way. For example, I've used programming as a marketer to manage search engine optimization and keyword research on business websites. I've also used my programming knowledge to write automated software tests.

Bottom line, programming becomes a tool in your problem-solving toolbox. This is the key to understanding how I approach this Scratch tutorial. I want the computer scientists to come along for the ride, but I'm catering to a broader audience.

Sample Scratch uses

I couldn't begin to suggest every possible way for you to use Scratch; that's why we have an imagination. However, here are a few ideas to get you started:

- Use Scratch to teach yourself or your students how to program. That's the obvious one.

- Use Scratch to demonstrate Math concepts. Scratch can also demonstrate the *x* and *y* coordinate system in an interactive way.

- Use Scratch to inspire your kids to read and write. Find a story and animate each scene or encourage them to animate the story. Turn their haiku into a Scratch project.

- Have a child who only wants to play video games? Make a deal. Your child can only play the games he creates or remixes with Scratch.

As you work through the examples in this book, write down your project ideas no matter how hard, easy, obvious, or silly they seem. The next one might be your best idea yet.

Computational thinking

Learning: we do it for life. We should help our children develop skills that will help them keep learning and solving problems in an increasingly digital environment. Using Scratch, we will learn how to design, think, collaborate, communicate, analyze, and program in a computer language.

You may frame the Scratch approach as computational thinking. According to Wikipedia:

> *Computational thinking is a problem solving method that uses computer science techniques. The term computational thinking was first used by Seymour Papert in 1996.*

By the time we make our cat dance for the first time, we'll forget all about the academic research and theories behind Scratch. Instead, we'll focus on having fun and creating the next project.

Finding a project for you

This book will give you a well-rounded introduction to Scratch. It's true that creating games are incredibly popular, and young boys tend to want to create games. However, there are other uses of Scratch, and plenty of people who want to do something other than just create games. Generally speaking, we'll make an animation, tell a story, build a game, create art, and sense the real world.

Making animations

An animation lets the sprites interact with each other. We'll use the common example of a birthday card to demonstrate animations. The following screenshot shows a birthday card example from *Chapter 3, Creaing an Animated Birthday Card*:

However, some folks have created more complicated projects using **stop-motion animations**. You can find some stop-motion animations on the Scratch website at `http://scratch.mit.edu/studios/254628/`.

Telling stories

The first story project we do will create a slideshow that's designed to be narrated with Scratch's built-in audio capabilities. The following screenshot is a preview of our slideshow:

Our second story project takes a more classical approach to tell a story by creating a book with a table of contents and then animating the individual scenes as a way of narrating the story.

Building games

Games are by the far the most popular Scratch project, and people tend to create all the normal types of games: platformer games, scrolling backgrounds, role-playing games, mazes, and classic arcade games. We'll remix the classic Pong game into a challenging game of Breakout, and in the process, we'll set the stage for many common game-programming concepts. The following screenshot shows the Breakout game:

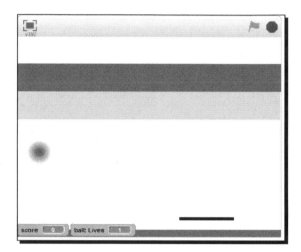

Programming games of chance

We will encounter randomness throughout the book, but we'll develop a project that applies random outcomes to an interactive story. The following screenshot shows a Trip to the fortune teller:

Creating art projects

The Scratch site is loaded with talented illustrators, and Scratch provides all the tools needed to draw characters and scenes, namely a paint editor and an easy way to animate them. The other kind of art you'll find on the Scratch site is computer-generated art, and we'll spend time drawing geometric shapes, as seen in the following screenshot:

Sensing the real world

Scratch has historically included support for add-on hardware, such as **PicoBoard** and **LEGO WeDo**. Scratch also includes built-in support to use the computer's webcam and senses external sounds using the computer's microphone. We'll explore the webcam, microphone, and PicoBoard in our project.

Programming concepts

The following table summarizes several programming concepts that can be learned with Scratch. It's included here primarily to reinforce Scratch as a programming language and foreshadow the concepts we'll use throughout the book. We'll introduce concepts in greater detail as we work through the book.

Concept	Description
Interface design	When we design a program, we turn our imagination into a creation that can be shared with others. We create the flow of the program, how the user interacts with the project, and the actions each sprite takes to tell our story.

Concept	Description
Loops (iteration)	A loop repeats (iterates) through a list of programming commands (also known as blocks in Scratch). Often, we'll use conditional statements to control when and how often a loop runs.
Boolean logic	A Boolean command evaluates a given statement as true or false. In Scratch, a Boolean command can check whether a specified condition is true (for example, is the color blue?), or we can compare values with and, or, and not operators. For example, if 4 > 0 and 4 < 2.
Variables	Variables store text or numbers for reuse in the program. For example, if x > 0 creates a conditional statement that evaluates whether the number assigned to x is greater than 0.
Arrays (Lists)	Arrays are similar to variables in that they store information that may or may not change. However, a list stores multiple values in the same way a grocery list stores a group of items.
Events	Scratch provides an entire group of event blocks that allows us to tell our program what to do when that event happens. For example, events include when flag is clicked or when a space key is pressed.
Synchronization and coordination	Programming a sprite to receive a broadcast message from another sprite coordinates a cause and effect. Broadcasting a message and waiting for all the other sprites to act on the broadcast synchronizes the action. Throughout the book, broadcasts are a technique we will use often, and they provide the fundamental communication between the sprites in the project.
Concurrency	Creating two scripts to run on the same control enables parallel execution. For example, programming four different sprites to pixelate when the green flag is clicked creates four concurrent actions.
Random numbers	This concept picks a random number from a specified range.
Cloud data	Scratch 2.0 introduces cloud variables that enable projects to store data on the Scratch web servers so that the data is available to other Scratch users. For example, the use of cloud data might include keeping a high score or tracking the survey results.
Procedures	Procedures can also be called as functions or methods in other programming languages. Scratch 2.0 adds the ability to create custom blocks that allows you to create a stack of blocks under a single name. When you use a custom block, you can pass an argument, such as a sprite number, into the procedure.
Vector and Bitmap graphics	Scratch includes a built-in image editor that enables you to create graphics and sprites for your projects. Vector graphics is a new feature of Scratch 2.0.

Concept	Description
Cloning	New to Scratch 2.0, cloning allows a sprite to duplicate itself while the program is running. Clones inherit the parent sprite's costumes and scripts. For example, many people create games that need to shoot something, such as asteroids. Cloning in Scratch 2.0 allows us to shoot multiple times.
Video	By using the computer's built-in webcam, Scratch 2.0 can enable the project to sense the video(s).

Using Scratch 2.0

With the release of Scratch 2.0, project creation has primarily moved online. For users who do not have access to the Internet, the Scratch team has launched a complementary offline editor. I'll introduce you to both the environments.

To get started, in your Flash-enabled web browser, go to `http://scratch.mit.edu`.

> For more information about installing Adobe Flash, go to `http://get.adobe.com/flashplayer/` in your web browser.

You'll get a page that resembles the following screenshot:

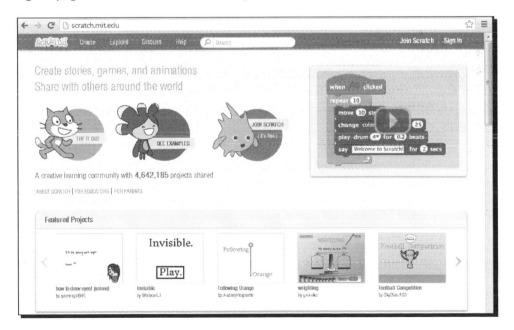

The top of the page contains the **Create**, **Explore**, and **Discuss** links. As we work through our projects, we'll spend our time creating projects, and I'll leave the forum discussions for later. For now, let's just look at a project.

At the time I wrote this chapter, the **Following Orange** project was displayed as a featured project. It's available at `http://scratch.mit.edu/projects/14852464/`. If for some reason this project is not available in the future, just click on any project on the Scratch home page and play it. Just experience a Scratch project as a user.

The following screenshot shows the **Following Orange** project:

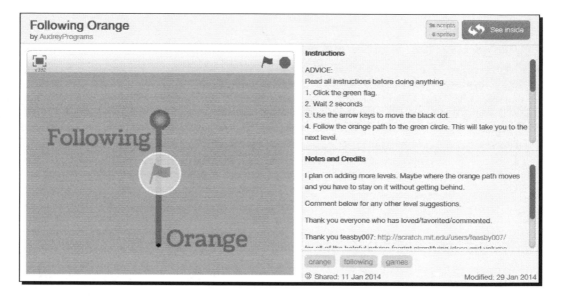

When you share your projects with the Scratch community, this is the primary view. It's a relatively intuitive design. The users provide some instructions and credits about the project as seen in the right-half of the previous screenshot. The project displays a green flag in a circle, and clicking on the green flag starts (initializes) the project.

Above the stage, we see the project name with the name of the author (I have no idea who this user is as I just selected it out of convenience). To the right of the project name is a blue **See inside** button. When you click on **See inside**, you'll see the project editor.

Looking inside a Scratch project

Clicking on the **See inside** button for a project will display the details of the project in the project editor, as seen in the following screenshot. If you click on the **Create** button from the Scratch website, you will open a new project in the same view.

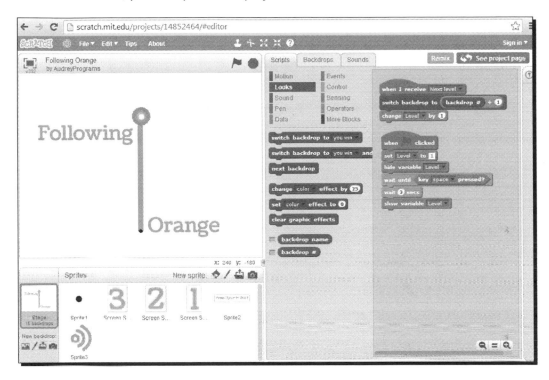

The display gets a little more complicated because there are more things available on the screen, but it's important to note that everything we need to create, test, and run our projects is accessible from the single view of the project editor.

To borrow a phrase from the Scratch Wiki, the project editor is divided into palettes and panes. At this point, I'll draw your attention to three key areas: the stage, the sprites pane, and the script area. Using the **Following Orange** project as a guide, we'll discuss each one of the three key areas in the following sections.

The stage area

The large space beneath the green flag and the stop sign icons is the **stage**. This is where our sprites act out their scripts. It's here that we get to see the result of our programming.

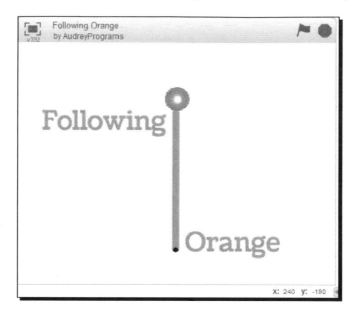

The sprites pane

Sprites are the characters and objects in our Scratch projects. The list of sprites can be found below the stage. The following screenshot shows the list of sprites available to the **Following Orange** project:

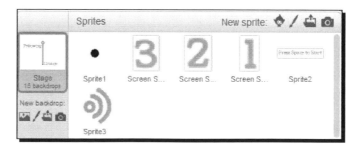

The scripts area

In order to get our sprites to animate, move, or interact with one another on the stage, we need to create one or more scripts for each sprite. If you click on a sprite from the list, the project editor will show the existing stacks of blocks in the scripts area.

A stack of blocks is a script, and a sprite can have multiple scripts assigned to it. In this book, I'll use either script or stack to refer to a collection of blocks.

The following screenshot shows a script for one of the sprites in the **Following Orange** project:

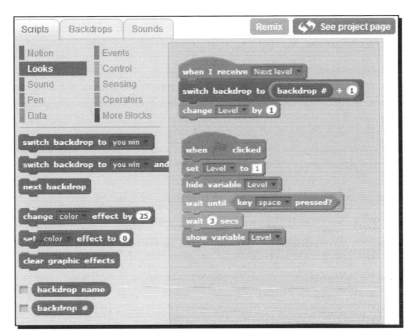

To create a game, story, or animation in Scratch, we stack blocks together to form a script that gives instructions to the project sprites. In the middle of the project editor screen, we have categories of blocks that are grouped by the kinds of tasks they represent. They are **Motion, Looks, Sound, Pen, Data, Events, Control, Sensing, Operators,** and **More Blocks.** Throughout the book, I'll refer to these categories of blocks as **palettes**; they can be seen in the previous screenshot.

The palettes of blocks are analogous to the palette of colors an artist mixes while creating a painting. We mix the blocks together to form our art work. Each type of block is color coded so that we can easily identify them by their type in our scripts.

The commands written on the blocks are in plain English, and they don't require a lot of effort to understand the basic idea behind any block. Take the script visible in the previous screenshot as an example. You might not know exactly what these two scripts do, but by reading the blocks, you will generally understand that these blocks are initializing the game and changing to the next level.

The built-in image editor

One of the core features of Scratch is its built-in image editor, which allows us to draw our own backgrounds and sprites. This makes it incredibly easy for users to create sprites and project backgrounds, and it's readily available from the project editor.

Previous versions of Scratch used a bitmap image editor, but as of Version 2.0, Scratch can also draw in vector graphics, which allows us to create images that are smooth and scalable to any size.

The following screenshot shows the default Scratch cat in the paint editor. If you've used any image editor in the past, including GIMP or Photoshop, then the drawing tools should have a familiar feel to them.

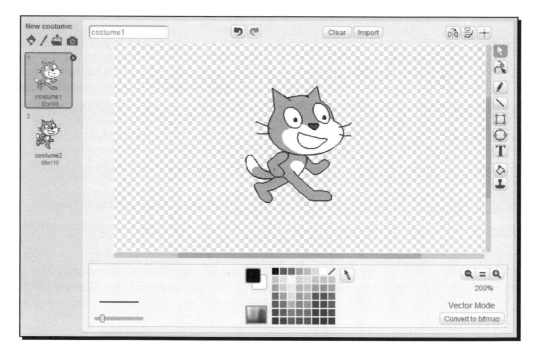

Scratch's built-in paint editor is relatively basic in terms of the number of features, but is functional for most of our uses. In general, the paint editor will allow you to perform the following tasks:

◆ Create shapes and text
◆ Import and edit images in popular formats
◆ Apply color
◆ Resize and change the orientation of the image

The image editor is available from multiple points within the Scratch interface, as we'll see throughout the book. We'll cover the paint editor in greater detail in *Chapter 3, Creating an Animated Birthday Card*.

Using Scratch 2.0 offline

It's not possible to be connected to the Internet all the time, which may be an increasingly difficult idea to accept for some people. Nevertheless, consider that your Internet connection may go down, that the Scratch website may be offline for updates, or perhaps your Internet connection is slow.

If you can't get to the Scratch website, then you can't create a project using the online project editor. Thankfully, the Scratch team has released an offline editor. You can download it from `http://scratch.mit.edu/scratch2download/`.

The download page includes an online installer that will install the prerequisite software, namely Adobe Air, on your computer. The following screenshot shows the **Scratch 2 Offline Editor**:

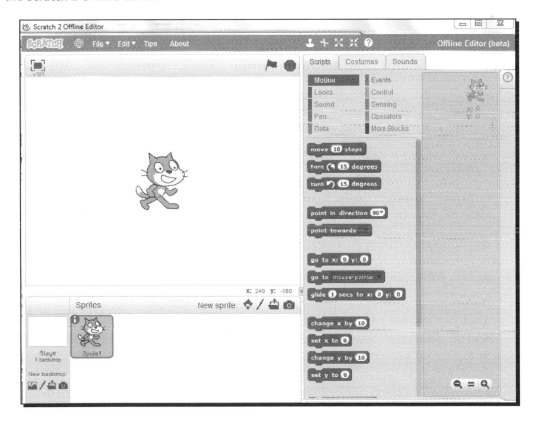

As we see, the offline editor looks like the online editor. Using the offline editor, you can create projects and then share them to the Scratch website. We'll review sharing projects in *Chapter 2, A Quick Start Guide to Scratch*. The offline version of Scratch 2.0 has been in development for several months following the official release of Scratch 2.0.

The previous screenshot indicates that the editor shown is **beta**. Be sure to double-check the download page for information pertaining to the functionality and release stability of the offline editor. I would highly recommend downloading the offline version as a backup to the online version. While the Scratch team does make a great effort to protect user privacy, creating and saving projects offline does not require an account on the Scratch website, ensuring user privacy.

Encountering Scratch 1.4

One of the biggest limiting factors of Scratch 2.0 is its reliance on Flash and Adobe Air (for the offline version). Not all computer systems are capable of running Flash environments; some Linux users and users of the low-cost, credit card-sized Raspberry Pi come to mind. The Pi is a Linux-based computer that's capable of plugging into an existing television set and keyboard. The Pi and Linux versions in general run Scratch 1.4. My XO laptop also runs Scratch 1.4.

All of these Flash challenges increase the likelihood of encountering Scratch 1.4. I do not insist on the use of Scratch 1.4 until we come across the PicoBoard projects in *Appendix A, Connecting a PicoBoard to Scratch 1.4*; however, if you're a Scratch 1.4 user, most of these projects can be adapted with little effort. I've taken the effort to specifically identify features that are exclusive to Scratch 2.0 so that users of the older versions can adapt appropriately.

Tinkering encouraged

The structure of the Scratch interface makes it easy for us to tinker and explore ideas. As we create projects, we evaluate our work and determine whether the results meet our expectations. It's very easy because everything happens in one interface.

To check whether our project works, we don't have to compile the code, switch windows, upload files to a server, or work around any number of other obstacles to run our project. Scratch enables us to modify the program as it runs and see the results in real time.

Summary

In this chapter, we reviewed Scratch both in terms of its possibilities and how it's used in the book to create stories, animations, games, and art. Whether you're a mom, a dad, a workshop facilitator, or a young scratcher, this chapter lays the foundation for the work we'll do in the rest of the book. We've even explored a project and the project editor.

In the next chapter, we'll create an online Scratch account, explore the community, and then move right into our first Scratch project. It'll give us an easy way to tinker with the Scratch interface and take our first steps. We'll focus on some project management fundamentals including naming objects, sharing projects, and lots of things in between.

2

A Quick Start Guide to Scratch

The anticipation of learning a new programming language can sometimes leave us frozen on the starting line, not knowing what to expect or where to start. Together, we'll take our first steps into programming with Scratch, and block-by-block, we'll create our first animation. Our work in this chapter will focus on getting ourselves comfortable with some fundamental concepts before we create projects in the rest of the book.

In this chapter, we will be introduced to Scratch programming. We will:

◆ Join and tour the online Scratch community

◆ Create a project to take our first steps in Scratch

◆ Introduce loops using forever and repeat blocks

◆ Add and animate multiple sprites in a project

◆ Remix a video-sensing project

Joining the Scratch community

If you're planning to work with the online project editor on the Scratch website, I highly recommend you set up an account on `scratch.mit.edu` so that you can save your projects. If you're going to be working with the offline editor, then there is no need to create an account on the Scratch website to save your work; however, you will be required to create an account to share a project or participate in the community forums.

Let's take a moment to set up an account and point out some features of the main account. That way, you can decide if creating an online account is right for you or your children at this time.

Time for action – creating an account on the Scratch website

Let's walk through the account creation process, so we can see what information is generally required to create a Scratch account. Open a web browser and go to `http://scratch.mit.edu`, and click on the link titled **Join Scratch**.

1. At the time of writing this book, you will be prompted to pick a username and a password, as shown in the following screenshot. Select a username and password. If the name is taken, you'll be prompted to enter a new username. Make sure you don't use your real name. This is shown in the following screenshot:

2. After you enter a username and password, click on **Next**. Then, you'll be prompted for some general demographic information, including the date of birth, gender, country, and e-mail address, as shown in the following screenshot. All fields need to be filled in.

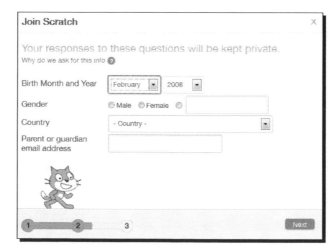

3. After entering all the information, click on **Next**. The account is now created, and you receive a confirmation screen as shown in the following screenshot:

4. Click on the **OK Let's Go!** button to log in to Scratch and go to your home page.

What just happened?

Creating an account on the Scratch website generally does not require a lot of detailed information. The Scratch team has made an effort to maximize privacy. They strongly discourage the use of real names in user names, and for children, this is probably a wise decision.

The birthday information is not publicized and is used as an account verification step while resetting passwords. The e-mail address is also not publicized and is used to reset passwords. The country and gender information is also not publically displayed and is generally just used by Scratch to identify the users of Scratch. For more information on Scratch and privacy, visit: http://scratch.mit.edu/help/faq/#privacy.

Time for action – understanding the key features of your account

When we log in to the Scratch website, we see our home page, as shown in the following screenshot:

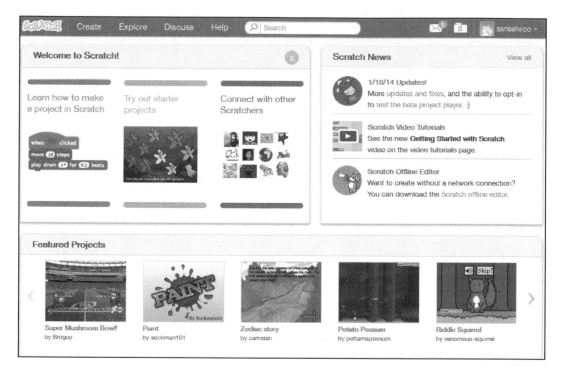

We reviewed the **Create** and **Explore** interfaces briefly in *Chapter 1, Welcome to Scratch 2.0*; so, we'll take a brief click-through tour of some of the primary features, starting from the right-hand side of the navigation and working towards the left.

> *1.* All the projects we create online will be saved to **My Stuff**. You can go to this location by clicking on the folder icon with the **S** on it, next to the account avatar, at the top of the page. The following screenshot shows my projects:

2. Next to the My Stuff icon in the navigation pane is **Messages**, which is represented by a letter icon. This is where you'll find notifications of comments and activity on your shared projects. Clicking on this icon displays a list of messages.

3. The next primary community feature available to the subscribed users is the **Discuss** page. The **Discuss** page shows a list of forums and topics that can be viewed by anyone; however, an account is required to be able to post on the forums or topics.

What just happened?

A Scratch account provides users with four primary features when they view the website: saving projects, sharing projects, receiving notifications, and participating in community discussions.

When we view our saved projects in the **My Stuff** page, as we can see in the previous screenshot, we have the ability to **See inside** the project to edit it, share it, or delete it.

 All newly created projects are unshared by default. Users will need to explicitly share the project for others to view it.

Abiding by the terms of use

It's important that we take a few moments to read the terms of use policy so that we know what the community expects from us. Taken directly from Scratch's terms of use, the major points are:

◆ Be respectful

◆ Offer constructive comments

◆ Share and give credit

◆ Keep your personal information private

◆ Help keep the site friendly

Creating projects under Creative Commons licenses

Every work published on the Scratch website is shared under the Attribution-ShareAlike license. That doesn't mean you can surf the web and use copyrighted images in your work. Rather, the **Creative Commons licensing** ensures the collaboration objective of Scratch by making it easy for anyone to build upon what you do.

When you look inside an existing project and begin to change it, the project keeps a remix tree, crediting the original sources of the work. A shout out to the original author in your projects would also be a nice way to give credit.

For more information about the Creative Commons Attribution-ShareAlike license, visit `http://creativecommons.org/licenses/by-sa/3.0/`.

Closely related to the licensing of Scratch projects is the understanding that you as a web user can not inherently browse the web, find media files, incorporate them into your project, and then share the project for everyone.

Respect the copyrights of other people. To this end, the Scratch team enforces the **Digital Millennium Copyright Act** (**DMCA**), which protects the intellectual rights and copyrights of others. More information on this is available at `http://scratch.mit.edu/DMCA`.

Finding free media online

As we'll see throughout the book, Scratch provides libraries of media, including sounds and images that are freely available for use in our Scratch projects. However, we may find instances where we want to incorporate a broader range of media into our projects.

A great search page to find free media files is `http://search.creativecommons.org`.

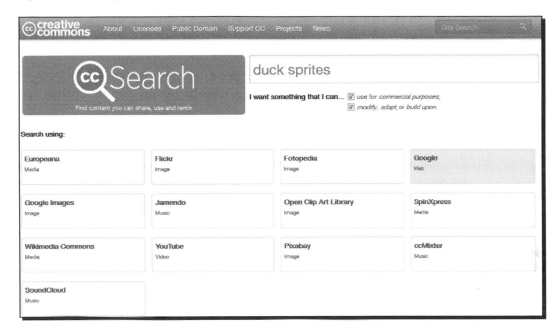

Taking our first steps in Scratch

From this point forward, we're going to be project editor agnostic, meaning you may choose to use the online project editor or the offline editor to work through the projects.

When we encounter software that's unfamiliar to us, it's common to wonder, "Where do I begin?". The Scratch interface looks friendly enough, but the blank page can be a daunting thing to overcome. The rest of this chapter will be spent on building some introductory projects to get us comfortable with the project editor.

If you're not already on the Scratch site, go to `http://scratch.mit.edu` and let's get started.

Time for action – moving the cat across the stage

As a warm up, we're going to make the default Scratch cat move across the stage.

1. Click on the **Create** button to open a new project in the editor. The project contains a single sprite—the Scratch cat.

2. In the blocks palette, click on the **Events** button.

3. Drag the **when flag clicked** block to the scripts.

4. In the blocks palette, click on the **Motion** button.

5. Drag the **move (10) steps** block to the scripts area and snap it to the bottom of the **when flag clicked** block, as shown in the following screenshot:

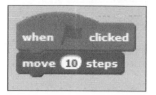

How to snap two blocks together

As you drag a block onto another block, a white line is displayed to indicate that the block you are dragging can be added to the script. When you see the white line, release your mouse to snap the block in place.

6. Click on the green flag above the stage repeatedly to set our first Scratch program in motion.

If the cat reaches the end of the stage, you need to manually move the sprite to the left side of the stage by clicking-and-dragging the cat.

What just happened?

Our first Scratch project combined two blocks to make the cat move across the screen. The first block we used was the **when flag clicked** block from the **Events** block, and, very simply, when the flag was clicked, we used the **move () steps** block to give the cat some motion.

As we clicked through the blocks palette, we saw that the available blocks changed depending on whether we chose **Motion**, **Looks**, or **Events**. Each set of blocks is color coded to help us easily identify them in our scripts.

Did you look closely at the blocks as you snapped them together? As children, most of us probably had a game where we needed to put the round peg into the round hole. Building a Scratch program is just that simple. We see instantly how one block may or may not fit into another block. One of the friendly design aspects of Scratch is that it's incredibly obvious when two blocks fit together, just like when you put puzzle pieces together or build with LEGO. Scratch's building block design is heavily influenced by LEGO. The **Events** block, for example, always sit on top of a stack of other blocks. You can never put the **move () steps** block on top of the **when flag clicked** block.

The **move (10) steps** block accepts a numeric value that can be changed. Throughout the book, we'll encounter many blocks that accept values, and often, the blocks have a default value, such as the move block. In the exercises, you will notice block values are kept in parenthesis, and sometimes you might see the block referenced with the value, as in **move (10) steps**. When we need to change the default value, you might see the block written in the format **move () steps**, which omits the default value.

Using events to trigger an action

One of the most important groups of blocks in Scratch is the **Events** block. We used the **when flag clicked** block as a trigger to make the cat move. There are other event blocks that we'll encounter in future projects, but a majority of the Scratch projects developed by the community will use the **when flag clicked** block to start the project.

As we develop more sophisticated projects, we'll see how the **when flag clicked** block can be used to initialize the starting values, positions, and views of the project.

Have a go hero – testing the move block

Take a minute to explore our two block scripts by changing the value in the **move () steps** block. Check what happens when you use a larger value such as 50 or a negative value such as -23.

Time for action – animating a walking motion with the cat

We're going to build on our script by creating an appearance of movement:

1. From the **Looks** palette, attach the **switch to costume ()** block to the **move ()** block in our script. The default costume will be **costume2**.

2. Click on the green flag to move the cat. Note that the first time we clicked on the flag, the appearance of the cat changed, but it remained the same on subsequent movements.

3. We'll make the animation more realistic in a minute, but let's examine the costumes by clicking on the **Costumes** tab. The following screenshot shows the contents of the **Costumes** tab:

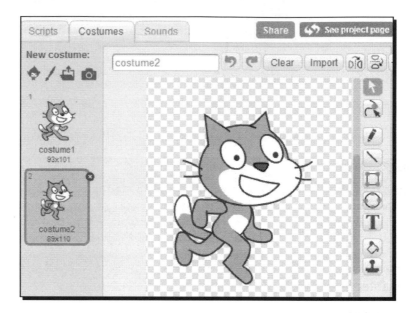

4. This view opens the sprite in the paint editor, but our primary interest is the costume thumbnails. If you've run the script as we've created, then **costume2** is highlighted. Alternatively, click on the thumbnails and observe how selecting the costume displays on the stage.

5. Depending on the speed of your clicks, the cat has the appearance of walking or running in place. There's no horizontal movement associated with toggling the costumes back and forth.

6. Now, let's adjust the script to replicate this walking motion. Add another **switch to costume ()** to our script. Select **costume1**.

7. Now, repeatedly click the green flag. You will discover that our script doesn't appear to switch the costumes like we expected.

8. Scratch is actually running our blocks faster than we can see with our naked eye. We need to adjust the timing so that we can see the animation. From the **Control** palette, snap a **wait () secs** block between the **switch to costume (costume1)** and **switch to costume (costume2)** blocks.

9. The default value in the **wait () secs** block is 1. Change it to a smaller number, such as **.2**, to speed up the time it takes to switch the costumes.

10. Our revised script can be seen in the following screenshot:

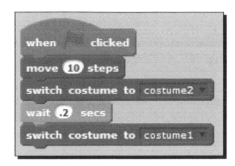

What just happened?

By adding the **switch costume to ()** blocks, our script now gives the appearance of walking. The **wait () secs** block added some timing so that the transition between the costumes could be detected.

Costumes are a fundamental part of Scratch and can be used to change the appearance of our sprite, as we've seen in our example. There's a limiting factor in our script so in that the cat only takes a step when the green flag is clicked.

We'll continue to refine the movement and action of our script, but let's pause for a moment to put our simple project into a wider Scratch context.

Understanding the basics of a Scratch Project

Inside every Scratch project, we will find the following ingredients: sprites, costumes, blocks, scripts, and a stage. It's how we mix the ingredients with our imagination that creates captivating stories, animations, and games. Think of each sprite in a Scratch program (also known as a project) as an actor. Each actor walks onto the stage and recites a script, which consists of individual lines. How each actor interacts with another actor depends on the words the director chooses, and we are in the director's seat of our Scratch programs.

Throughout the book, we'll learn how to add and customize sprites. A sprite wears a costume like an actress dresses up for her role in the play. Change the costume, and you change the way the sprite looks. Blocks are commands that are grouped by their type and include **Motion, Looks, Sound, Pen, Data, Events, Control, Sensing, Operators**, and **More Blocks**. We snap blocks together to create scripts, as our current exercises demonstrate.

Scripts are a set of blocks that tell a sprite exactly what to do. Each block represents an instruction or a piece of information that contributes to the sprite or to the project in general. We'll explore those relationships in our projects.

Saving early, often, and automatically

It's good practice to get in the habit of saving our work.

Time for action – saving our work

The online project editor will autosave our work, but it's good practice to manually save our projects, especially before you close your web browser or navigate away from the Scratch website.

1. To manually save your new project, click on **Save now** from the **File** menu at the top of the project editor. This works whether we're working with the online or offline editor.

2. As you review the project, you'll notice that each project has a name. Our current project is called **untitled**. To change the name of your project from **untitled**, find the white textbox above the stage and change the project name to something meaningful by clicking in the box and typing. The following screenshot shows the project name in relation to the screen. My project is named **run, kitty, run**.

What just happened?

Autosave is nice and will generally limit our loss should we encounter an unexpected error or loss of Internet connectivity. The general rule whenever you're creating something is to save early and save often. This is especially true for users of the offline editor, where there is no autosave feature.

A variation of saving the current project is to use **Save as a copy** to create a copy of the current project. This is useful if we want to save our work at a particular point. There is no versioning within Scratch, so sometimes saving a copy of a project before making a lot of additional changes is the only reliable way to get back to a known starting point.

Undoing a deletion

If you deleted something you shouldn't have, there is an **Undelete** option under the **Edit** menu at the top of the Scratch editor. You can only undelete the most recent item that you deleted.

Introducing forever loops

Let's get back to our walking cat animation and set it in perpetual motion. When we do something forever, we constantly repeat it. In Scratch's context, forever means we're going to constantly loop through a series of blocks for as long as the project is running.

Time for action – setting the cat in motion, forever

So far, the cat has moved incrementally across the screen each time we clicked the green flag. Now, we're going to introduce the idea that the cat can stay in motion forever.

1. We want to wrap the stack of blocks in a forever block. To do this, click on the **move (10) steps** block in the script and detach it from the **when flag clicked**.

2. Now, from the **Control** palette, snap the **forever** block onto the **when flag clicked** block. Grab the stack of blocks you detached and drag it to the center of the **forever** block. Your script should look like the following screenshot:

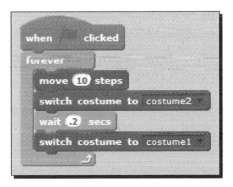

3. Run the script and watch the cat disappear from the stage.

4. Let's get the runaway cat back. From the **Motion** palette, add the **if on edge, bounce** block to the bottom of the **forever** block. Now, watch the cat reappear upside down and bounce around the bottom-right corner of the stage.

5. To stop the cat, click once on the script or click on the stop sign above the stage.

The following screenshot shows the current state of our project:

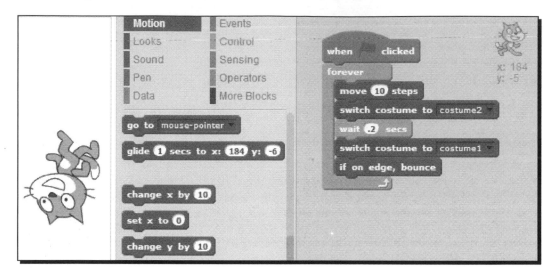

Our script has a couple of issues to work through, such as a choppy walking motion and an upside down cat. We'll come back and fix this up some more, but first let's consider what we accomplished.

What just happened?

We wrapped our entire script in a **forever** block, which is synonymous with a **loop**. In programming, a loop runs a group of commands over and over again. After we repeatedly instructed the sprite to move across the stage, it didn't take long before it went off the stage.

The **if on edge, bounce** block did as the name implies—it turned the cat around when it hit the edge of the stage. As the **if on edge, bounce** block was the last block in the forever loop, the script checked for the edge of the stage with each step.

If you carried out the steps in the exercise as described, you will see that as soon as you placed the **if on edge, bounce** block into your script, the sprite reappeared.

 You can add blocks to the loop and change the block attributes as the script runs, and the sprite automatically adjusts to the new values.

Controlling a sprite with loops

Any time we need to repeat an action within a project, we use a loop. The **forever** block represents an infinite loop because there is nothing in the script that tells the block to stop running. The blocks inside the loop will run as long as the Scratch program is running. We'll use loops throughout the book to control how a sprite behaves and to continually evaluate the changing conditions of our games, stories, and animations.

Time for action – flipping the cat right-side up

Let's tweak our script so the cat rotates right-side up and see if we can speed up our steps:

1. Scratch 2.0 introduced the **set rotation style** block in the **Motion** palette that will set our cat right-side up. From the **Motion** palette, find the **set rotation style ()** block and add it to your script after the **set rotation style ()** block. The default attribute for the set rotation block is **left-right**, which fixes our problem.

2. Click on the stack of blocks to run the script. Your script should look like the following screenshot:

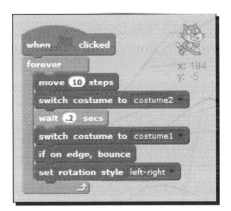

3. Now, let's address the choppy movement of the sprite. From the **Looks** palette, drag the **next costume** block into the scripts area. Don't attach it to the script yet because we want to expose another one of Scratch's features. If the cat is still moving, you can stop it by clicking the stop sign.

4. Click the **next costume** block directly. And then, repeatedly click on the block so that you see the cat switching between its costumes with each click of the block. This block is mimicking the functionality we've already built into the script, but we'll explain the full ramifications after we wrap up the exercise.

5. Remove the following blocks from the script by clicking on them and dragging them to an empty spot in the scripts area: **switch costume to (costume2)**, **wait (.2) secs**, and **switch costume to (costume1)**.

 Removing blocks from the middle of the script is not always a clean process. Often, Scratch will remove more blocks than you want it to. As long as you drag the blocks to the Scripts area, you can easily add the relevant blocks back to the script.

6. Add the **next costume** block after the **move (10) steps** block, replacing the three blocks we just removed. Verify your script against the following screenshot:

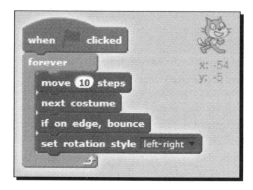

What just happened?

Of primary interest to us was getting the cat's rotation correct as it bounced off the edge of the stage. The **set rotation style (left-right)** block told the cat to rotate horizontally. Before we set the **rotation**, the cat was flipping vertically as it reversed direction.

The next thing we did was consolidate the changing of the costumes down to a single next costume block. This made the running motion smoother but much faster. We can slow the cat back down by adding a **wait () secs** block at the end of the forever loop and experimenting with values.

You might be wondering why we were able to replace the multiple **switch costume to ()** blocks with **next costume** and still see the running motion of the cat. The reason lies in the loop. Before we added the forever loop, the script used two blocks to explicitly switch between the costumes. These two **switch costume to ()** blocks equaled one step. The **wait (.2) secs** block put a slight hesitation in the step. In order to get the appearance of running or walking, we needed to manually switch between the two costumes within that one step.

When we replaced the **switch costume to ()** blocks with a single next costume block, each step was now a costume switch. The animation was much smoother even without the **wait () secs** block. All the blocks in the loop became one step that was repeated forever. The continual looping of the script provided the same end result that we had when we added the multiple **switch costume to ()** blocks.

With the **next costume** block, we don't need to know the name of the costume or even care how many costumes the sprite has. If the current costume is number one, then the next time through the loop, the costume will change to number two, and so on. When we use next costume, we do have to be concerned that the costumes fit the project we're working on.

On the other hand, if we need to explicitly display a sprite's costume, the **switch costume to ()** block is a better choice. For example, if we need to make sure a sprite looks a certain way at the start of a game, we'd use the **switch costume to ()** block in a script that started with **when flag clicked**.

Clicking on a block runs the command

Before we added the **next costume** block to the script, we placed it in the scripts area and clicked on the block. This allowed us to run the block before we added it to the script and is a feature of Scratch. Until this point, we've been clicking on the green flag to run the script, but we could just as easily be clicking on the stack of blocks to start to run the script.

The ability to run an individual block against a sprite gives us a chance to observe the behavior of the block before we add the block to our script. It's a great way to test and learn.

Have a go hero – exploring sprite rotation

The **set rotation style ()** block we used in our script has three rotation values available: **left-right**, **all around**, and **don't rotate**. Explore the behavior of the cat by using each rotation style.

Adding sprites to the project

So far, we have learned that if we want something done in Scratch, we must tell a sprite to act by creating one or more scripts. Scratch always starts a new project with a single cat. However, we don't always want to use the cat, and our games and stories will most likely include multiple sprites.

We can add sprites to the stage in one of the four ways: paint a new sprite, choose a sprite from the library, upload a sprite from file, or a new sprite from the camera. The icons to insert a sprite using one of these four methods are located in the **New sprite** pane, between the stage and the sprites list. The following screenshot shows the **New sprite** icons. Move the mouse over each icon to see a tooltip that identifies the new sprite method.

As we build future projects, we'll explore the various ways to add sprites. For now, we'll focus on Scratch's built-in sprite library. It's a great benefit to have a library of available sprites at the click of a mouse. The following screenshot shows what you see when you select the **choose sprite from library** option:

Time for action – adding a second sprite and script

We've mentioned that we can have multiple sprites acting out their scripts, but now we're going to add a second sprite to the project to illustrate the concept and explore some additional motion blocks and loops.

1. Add a new sprite by clicking on the **Choose new sprite from library** option. Then, browse to the **Animals** category and select **Dog1**. Click on **OK** to add the dog to the project.

2. Ensure **Dog1** is selected in the sprite list to ensure we have the scripts area for the dog.

3. From the **Motion** palette, drag one of the **turn** blocks into the scripts area.

Two turn blocks

If you look in the **Motion** palette, you'll notice that there are two turn blocks. One has a circle arrow that points clockwise and the other **turn** block points counter-clockwise.

4. Find the **repeat** block from the **Control** palette and snap it around the **turn** block.

5. Wrap the script in the **forever** block.

6. From the **Events** palette, add the **when this sprite clicked** block on top of the entire stack of blocks.

7. From the **Looks** palette, snap the **say () for () secs** block onto the bottom of the **repeat ()** block and above the **forever** block.

8. Next, we'll fine-tune the values of the blocks we just added. Change the value on the **repeat** block to **100**. Change the value on the **turn** block to **30**. Change the value on the **say** block to `chasin' my tail`.

9. Click on the dog on the stage and watch the sprite spin in a circle as if it's chasing its tail. Click on the green flag and set the cat on its trip back and forth across the stage.

The following screenshot shows the dog and its script:

What just happened?

We have two sprites on the screen that act independently of each other. This seems simple enough, but let's step through our script.

We added the dog sprite to the project and created a script that made the dog appear as if it was chasing its tail. Changing the value of the **turn** block will make the dog spin slower or faster.

By increasing or decreasing the value of the **repeat** block, we can control how many times the dog spins before it says **chasin' my tail**. The **repeat () blocks** contained in the repeat loop run for the number of times specified.

The repeat loop differs from the forever loop in that a repeat loop has a specified end, while the forever loop runs infinitely. As our exercise demonstrates, we can combine the loops, thereby providing multiple control points in our script.

Our exercise also introduced the idea of using multiple events in the same project to control when a sprite acts. The cat acts when the flag is clicked, while the dog acts only when you click on the dog sprite.

Reviewing a video-sensing project

We're going to leave our first Scratch project behind, and go out to the Scratch website to find a project that uses some of the blocks we've used throughout this chapter. Our main purpose is to view a complementary project in terms of blocks that can give us some ideas to extend our introductory project and introduce a Scratch 2.0 feature.

Time for action – reviewing pop the balloon - video starter

We'll be viewing a project from the Scratch website, so open a browser and go to http://scratch.mit.edu/projects/10126867/. Alternatively, you can download the book's supporting code files and open Pop the balloon - video starter.sb2. The project is from *chrisg*, a Scratch team member.

1. When you have the Pop the balloon - video starter.sb2 project open, click on the **See Inside** button to see the sprites and scripts of the project. If you're using the offline editor, you'll automatically open the project in the code view.

2. This program uses a webcam, so let's see what it does. Click on the green flag to start it.

3. You will be prompted with a message that indicates that Scratch wants access to your microphone and webcam. Click on **Allow**.

4. The view of your webcam is now on the Scratch stage with floating balloons. Touch the balloons to pop them.

5. This project has one sprite with two scripts. If you take a look at the script that begins when the flag is clicked on the block, most of these blocks look familiar, and that's why we're looking at this script at this point in time.

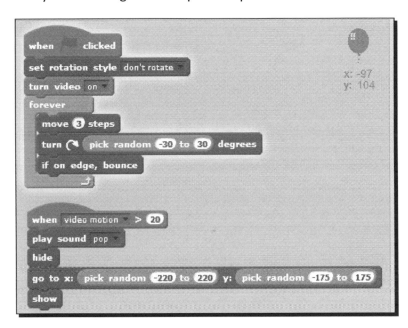

Downloading the example code

You can download the example code files for all Packt books you have purchased from your account at http://www.packtpub.com. If you purchased this book elsewhere, you can visit http://www.packtpub.com/support and register to have the files e-mailed directly to you.

What Just happened?

In our earlier chapter exercises, we've used the **set rotation style ()**, **forever**, **move () steps**, **turn () degrees**, and **if on edge, bounce** blocks to animate the cat and dog. In the balloon project, these same blocks are moving a balloon around the stage and creating a different effect, essentially by changing the values assigned to the blocks.

The biggest difference we see is the **pick random () to ()** block, which resides in the **Operators** palette. This block takes two values, which correspond to a range, meaning the **turn** block is randomly picking a number between -30 and 30. That gives the balloon the variation in the movement and gets it traveling up, down, right, and left. We'll encounter the **pick random () to ()** block again.

Sensing video

One of the other reasons for opening this project is that it demonstrates one of Scratch 2.0's features—**video sensing**. This feature has a lot of eye candy because it incorporates live video from the web cam into the project. However, we can't actually record videos for playback. It's limited to sensing motion and direction.

We're not going to work with video sensing in any of our future projects. Now that you know this feature, I recommend you explore video sensing after you learn some more of the basics behind Scratch programming.

Have a go hero – remixing ideas with our starter project

The one thing about learning to program with Scratch (or any language) is that sometimes you can use scripts, snippets, and ideas from another project to accomplish a task in your project. Can you take the motion of the balloon project and apply it to the cat in the starter project? Likewise, now that you have the video-sensing project open, you can take a stab at customizing in some way. We haven't covered much to this point, but there's nothing stopping you from a bit of exploration.

Pop quiz – getting started with Scratch

Q1. What are the advantages of registering an account with the Scratch website?

1. Ability to save and share projects from the online project editor.
2. Ability to post to the site forums.
3. Ability to save unshared projects in **My Stuff**.
4. All of the above.

Q2. Which one of the following blocks represents an event?

1. **move (15) steps**.
2. **when flag clicked**.
3. **repeat**.
4. **forever**.

Q3. Why would you use a **forever** block?

1. To run a series of commands for a set number of times.
2. To run a group of blocks only when a condition is true.
3. To run a group of blocks for as long as the project runs.
4. There is no good reason to use a **forever** block.

Q4. The **repeat ()** block does what?

1.   Runs a group of blocks for the specified number of times.

2.   Runs a group of block forever.

3.   Runs a stack of blocks each time the green flag is clicked on.

4.   Runs a stack of blocks each time the script is clicked on.

Q5. The repeat and forever blocks represent what programming concept?

1.   Variables.

2.   Loops.

3.   Events.

4.   Synchronization.

Summary

In this chapter, we covered a lot of ground and got a quick introduction to creating our first project in Scratch. We focused on moving the sprite around the stage. We made the cat travel across the stage continuously using a forever loop while the dog chased its tail. We learned that sprites can have multiple costumes, and when we create a script to access those costumes, we can animate the sprite's behavior.

In the next chapter, we will animate a birthday card, and in the process, we will learn to use Scratch's built-in paint editor. We'll also apply graphical effects and continue to work with events to ensure we get the time of our animations just right.

3

Creating an Animated Birthday Card

Now that we've taken a tour of Scratch and created some sample scripts,
let's actually create a complete project, right from concept to completion.
In this chapter, we will create an animated birthday card for a friend or
family member using both sprites that we design and sprites that we import
from Scratch's library. Animating a card is an excellent introductory Scratch
programming exercise because it can be accomplished using relatively basic
concepts. We'll also be introducing Scratch's paint editor in this chapter,
which gives really young children who might not be able to read very well
a low-tech way to interact with Scratch by drawing and editing sprites.

In addition to doing something fun, practical, and thoughtful, we will also learn how to:

- ◆ Design bitmap and vector images using the built-in paint editor
- ◆ Initialize a sprite's starting values
- ◆ Name sprites in easy-to-remember ways
- ◆ Transform sprites using graphical effects, loops, and broadcasts

We'll fill in these general ideas with details as we move through the exercises in this chapter.

Introducing the paint editor

Traditional birthday cards that you buy five minutes before a party are an impersonal way to show someone you care. So, when you care enough to send a card, make it a homemade card that you have designed yourself. Instead of cutting, gluing, and stenciling paper, we're going to make a homemade animated birthday card using Scratch.

Can't think of anyone to send a card to? Send it to yourself—I won't tell anyone.

Time for action – painting a happy birthday sprite

When we create a new project, our first task is to add our cast of characters and props; otherwise, we won't have any sprites to animate. Let's start by adding the most obvious part of a birthday card—the Happy Birthday text:

1. To start a new project, click on the **Create** button on the Scratch website.

2. We won't be using the cat, so you can delete that sprite by right-clicking on the cat icon, labeled as **Sprite1** in the sprites list, and choosing **delete**.

3. For our first sprite, we want to draw a new one; so, click on the Paint new sprite icon, as shown in the following screenshot:

4. Clicking on the Paint new sprite icon creates a new sprite named **Sprite1** and opens the paint editor to an empty canvas, as shown in the following screenshot. To start, click on the Text tool, as shown in the following screenshot, so that we are able to type:

5. Click on the canvas with your mouse where you want to type, and you'll see a vertical bar appear, which indicates that you are able to type. Go ahead and type `Happy Birthday`. If the text scrolls off the screen, use the horizontal and vertical scroll bars on the editor window to position the text in the editor window.

6. Don't like the default font? We can change it. Highlight the text you just typed and look at the bottom of the paint editor to find the **Font** menu. You can select from a limited number of fonts. In the following screenshot, I have selected the **Scratch** font:

7. As you can see, there is also a color palette available, so let's change the text color. Highlight the text and click on the color you want from the color palette. Happy Birthday is now displayed in the color you select.

8. If you're happy with the words, font, and color, you can save your sprite by clicking anywhere on the stage or the paint editor. The sprite is now visible on the stage. But be careful; after you click out of the Text tool, you will not be able to change your text.

> **Erasing mistakes**
>
> The toolbar contains an erase tool with an adjustable eraser width that allows you to remove parts of your image. If you want to change the words, font, or color of the text we just created, you'll need to erase the sprite and start over.

What just happened?

We used the default bitmap editor to create a simple Happy Birthday sprite in the font and color of our choice. Note that after we saved our text by clicking anywhere in the image editor or the stage, we created a sprite. Even though our sprite initially comprised of 13 letters, it's now treated as a single bitmap image instead of individual letters. If we need to change the details of the Happy Birthday sprite, we'll need to erase what we have created and start over again.

Changing the size of a bitmap image

After we save the size of our sprite, Scratch 2.0 does not provide a size setting in the bitmap version of the editor where we just created this image. Bitmap is the type of image we created in the previous exercise, and we'll talk a bit more about it in the following section.

To change the size of the sprite we just created, we can manually resize the image using the Grow and Shrink buttons, which are located directly above the flag and stop sign in the project editor. To manually make a sprite bigger, click on the Grow button and then on the sprite. The following screenshot shows the location of the Grow and Shrink buttons. Scratch will remember these sizes unless we change the size of the sprite with a block.

We can also change the size of the sprite by adding the **set size to ()** block from the **Looks** palette. The next exercise will use the **set size to ()** block.

Our exercise is focused on drawing a sprite using words; however, you can draw shapes or characters if you're so inclined.

Choosing bitmap or vector images

Not only does Scratch have a built-in image editor, but it also allows you to choose from bitmap or vector graphics. Bitmap images tend to be easier to work with, but as you make the image bigger in size, it becomes less clear and more blurry, and the quality deteriorates. The image appears to have rough edges. That's because a bitmap image is represented on a computer by pixels or single dots of color that are arranged in a pattern to create the image we see.

If we were to zoom in on a bitmap image, we would eventually see the individual dots. When we resize an image to the point where we start to see the individual pixels, this effect is commonly referred to as **pixilation**. The image is no longer smooth and crisp.

Vector graphics, on the other hand, will appear to be smooth no matter how big you make the images. However, they tend to be a bit harder to work with. When a vector graphic is displayed on a computer screen, a program (Scratch in this case) renders the image based on a mathematical calculation to draw the curves and lines instead of individual pixels of color. This makes the image scalable to any size while avoiding pixilation.

Let's try a side-by-side comparison using the Happy Birthday sprite.

Time for action – drawing a vector image

Let's draw the Happy Birthday sprite in the vector mode. Then, we'll increase the size of both our images to compare the appearance:

1. Create a new sprite by clicking on the Paint new sprite icon.

2. Convert the image to vector graphics by clicking on the **convert to vector** button at the bottom-right of the editor. When the mode changes, the toolbar moves to the right side of the editor.

3. From the toolbar, use the text tool to create a second Happy Birthday sprite.

4. Now, let's make the sprites bigger. From the **Looks** palette, drag the **set size to ()** block into the **Scripts** area. Change the size attribute to **300** and then click on the block to apply the size.

5. Repeat step 4 for the other Happy Birthday sprite we created.

6. View the project in fullscreen mode by clicking on the blue square located at the top of the stage, to the left of the project name. The output looks similar to the following screenshot:

When the project opens in fullscreen mode, the output on your screen should resemble the following screenshot:

As you can see in the previous screenshot, the image at the top is starting to pixelate and is not as crisp as the bottom sprite. This top image is the bitmap image.

What just happened?

In the preceding screenshot, the first Happy Birthday sprite is the bitmap image. As we made the sprites bigger by viewing the project in fullscreen mode, the bitmap starts to show ragged edges that didn't show up when we viewed the sprite in the editor at its original size. If you compare this bitmap image with the vector graphic, by comparison, the vector graphic looks smooth. Visually, that's the key difference between vector and bitmap graphics.

 In addition to creating your own vector images, the Scratch sprite library contains many vector-based images. The editor cannot convert bitmaps to vector images, and all imported images are imported as bitmaps.

You can choose to use vector or bitmap images depending on your ability and needs. The best way to find some Scratch drawing inspiration is to explore the community.

Changing the size of the vector image

When we create a vector image, Scratch allows us to resize the image by clicking on one of the control points on the boundary of the image. The following screenshot shows eight square control points around the Happy Birthday sprite that allow us to resize or reshape the image:

Of course, we can also change the size of the vector-based sprite by using the Grow or Shrink buttons and the **set size to ()** block, as discussed with the bitmap images.

Reviewing the image editing tools

Each image mode contains a toolbar. The following table defines the tools for both bitmap and vector modes. The tool name column corresponds to the tooltip you get when you hover your mouse over the tool.

The bitmap editing tools along with their descriptions are listed as follows:

Bitmap editing tools	Description
Brush	This tool is used to draw freehand. You can select a color and a line width.
Line	This tool is used to draw straight lines only by clicking-and-dragging the mouse on the canvas. You can select a color and line width.
Rectangle	This tool is used to draw a rectangle. In addition to selecting a line width and color, you can draw a solid rectangle or transparent rectangle.
Ellipse	This tool is used to draw an oval. In addition, you can hold down the *Shift* key to draw a circle with your mouse. You can draw an image with a solid or transparent center. You can also select a color and line width.
Text	This tool creates a text box with a cursor when you click on the canvas. You can select the font and color. However, the text can't be changed after you save it.
Fill with color	This tool fills a region with a solid color or gradient.
Erase	This tool enables an eraser with a selectable size. As you move the eraser over the canvas, it removes the image.
Select	This tool, as the name suggests, selects an area of the image that you can move, stretch, or shrink.
Select and duplicate	This tool selects an area of an image and then copies the selected area so that it can be dragged to a new place on the canvas.

The vector editing tools along with their descriptions are as follows:

Vector editing tools	Description
Select	This tool selects a sprite by clicking on it so that you can reposition or rotate it. It allows you to resize, shrink, or stretch the image.
Reshape	This tool changes the shape by clicking on and dragging one of the control points.
Pencil	This tool is used to draw a freehand design using a selectable line width and color.

Vector editing tools	Description
Line	This tool is used to draw a straight line on the canvas by clicking-and-dragging from one point to another. You can select the line width and color. To make a curvy line, you will first start with a straight line and then use the reshape tool to create the shape you need.
Rectangle	This tool is used to draw a rectangle. In addition to selecting a line width and color, you can draw a solid rectangle or transparent rectangle.
Ellipse	This tool is used to draw an oval, or hold down the *Shift* key to draw a circle with your mouse. You can draw an image with a solid or transparent center. Select a color and line width.
Color a shape	This tool is used to fill a vector object. Unlike the fill tool in the bitmap editor, it cannot fill a blank background or object.
Duplicate	This tool is used to select and copy an object with the mouse pointer. The copied object can then be moved and changed as needed.

Erasing in the vector mode

You may notice that there is no erase tool in the vector mode. In the vector mode, you can remove the sections of a line or curve by pressing the *Shift* key and clicking on a circle control point, or you can do this by dragging a control point to reshape the line. This functionality is available under the reshape tool. The following screenshot shows Gobo, one of Scratch's default sprites in the paint editor, with the reshape tool selected. Note the circular control points around the perimeter of the selected shape.

If you click around the Happy Birthday vector sprite we created, you'll also notice that it's possible to change the individual letters of the text we created as well as the color.

Filling the stage with color

A white background seems boring, and we're not about to tolerate boring, are we? Let's see how easy it is to design our stage with colors and gradients.

Time for action – using the fill with color tool to paint the stage

In this exercise, we're going to create a solid background for our card and add a border to the design using a second color. Before you paint the background, let's delete the bitmap version of the Happy Birthday sprite. Let's paint by performing the following steps:

1. Select **Stage** in the sprite list.

2. Select the **Backdrops** tab. Our project is new, so we see the default white background in the paint editor.

3. Apply a color by selecting the Color the shape tool and then choosing a color from the color palette. Click on the stage to fill it with the selected color.

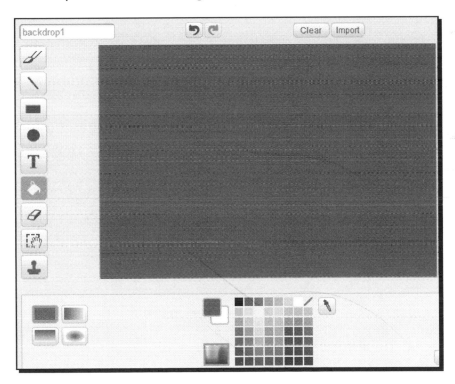

> **Undo**
>
> If you don't like the color you put in place, you can remove it by pressing the **Clear** button located above the editor. Likewise, you can use the Undo button, which is the counter-clockwise arrow.

4. Let's create a frame around the edge of the stage so that we can add a second color. Convert the stage backdrop to the vector mode so we can use the Rectangle tool.

5. Select the Rectangle tool and pick a contrasting color. Click on the image editor to draw a rectangle. The following screenshot shows a sample backdrop border on the stage:

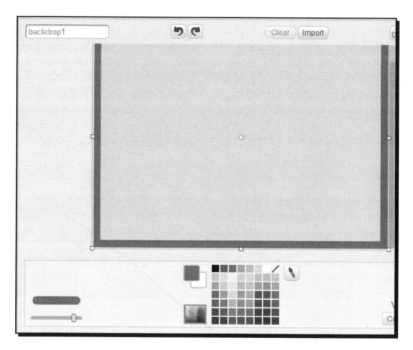

> **Changing the width of the line**
>
> At the bottom-left of the paint editor, there is a slider to control the width of the rectangle line. Several other tools also include a way to set the width of the line, including the pencil, line, ellipsis, rectangle, and reshape tools.

We've now given our stage some color and a touch of personality. Feel free to experiment here.

What just happened?

A basic tool of any image editing software is the fill tool, which allows you to fill an area with color. When we were working in the vector mode, our fill tool was called Color a shape. In the bitmap mode, it's called Fill with color. When we add the simple rectangle shape, we are able to create a border or a frame.

This exercise, beyond adding some color, should get you thinking about design. Even the simplest of projects will be designed. Our design is relatively simple right now. We have multiple colors and shapes in addition to the text.

One of the beautiful things about design (much like any other creative process) is that it's an iterative process, which means you expect to change it as the project evolves.

Adding gradients

Gradients gradually blend two colors together and are available in both the color a shape and Fill with color tools. Let's take a quick look at using the gradient tool.

Time for action – applying a gradient

In our previous exercise, we used the Color a shape tool to apply a solid color to the stage. Let's see what happens when we choose a gradient instead:

1. Open the stage in the paint editor if it's not already open. Then, select the color a shape tool.

2. Next to the color palette at the bottom of the editor are two color squares, one overlaid on top of the other. You can bring the bottom square to the front by clicking on it. Clicking on a color square from the palette will assign that color to the top square. Select two colors; we'll use them to draw a gradient.

3. Now select a gradient, which are the four squares available at the bottom left of the editor. The first option is the solid fill and working clockwise, we have horizontal, circular, and vertical. Choose one of the other gradient options and click on the image editor. Now, try reversing your two colors and see how the gradient changes.

4. The following screenshot shows a gradient along with the color options at the bottom of the editor:

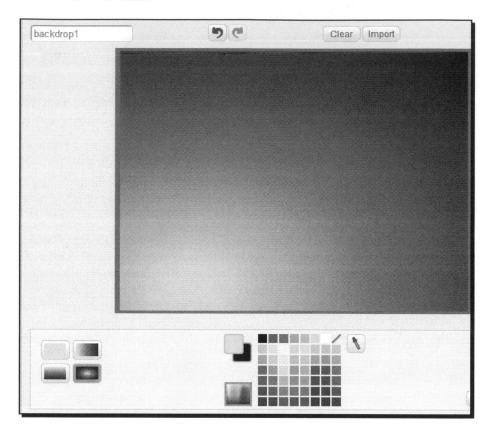

5. Now that you have a gradient option, you may choose to continue designing your card with it. For my card, I'm sticking to a solid background.

What just happened?

If you click around the stage and apply different gradients, one of the things you will notice is that color one is darkest at the point where you click onto the stage and then it gradually fades into the second color.

There are three gradient options. A vertical gradient will start with color one at the top of the stage and gradually fade into the second color. A horizontal gradient starts with the first color to the left of the stage and transitions to the second color as it fills to the right of the stage. Use the **flip left-right** and **flip up-down** options in the paint editor to change that orientation. The circular gradient starts wherever you click on the stage with color one and transitions to the second color as the circle reaches the edge of the stage.

While working with gradients, the gradient will fill to a boundary created by another line or shape. If the stage is empty, then the gradient will fill the entire space. If you draw a square in the middle of the stage and fill the square with a gradient, the gradient confines itself to the boundary of the square.

Time for action – adding more sprites to address the card

So far, we have not placed one block of code in our birthday card. This will change soon enough, but we have some additional sprites to add.

For this exercise, use the paint editor to spell out the name of the person receiving the card, but do it such that each letter is an individual sprite. This will give us more control over the animation of the name:

1. Use the Paint new sprite option one by one to create a sprite for each letter of the person who you are sending the card to. I'm sending my card to my mom, so I'm going to spell **Mom**. You may choose anyone you want, but I'd recommend you keep the name short for this exercise.

2. After you add the sprites, reposition the name on the stage by clicking and dragging each letter around the stage so that they form a word. If the letters are too small, you can resize them as needed.

3. The following screenshot shows my updated project. Note that I have three new sprites: **M**, **o**, and **m**.

What just happened?

Happy Birthday, Mom. Now it's starting to look like a card. For the grammarians among us, feel free to insert a comma after Birthday.

Did you make an observation as you dragged each letter around the stage to correctly spell mom? You dragged the M, the o, and the m independently of one another. We can't drag each letter in the Happy Birthday sprite around the stage. Go ahead, give it a try. You can move the entire phrase, but you cannot separate Happy from Birthday.

This subtle but important difference is what allows us to control the animation of each letter in the word mom, whereas in the Happy Birthday sprite, we can only control the entire phrase.

Initializing a sprite's starting values

As we animate the card, we need to start thinking about how the card looks when we give it to somebody. In other words, we need to know what happens when that person clicks on the green flag to view the card.

Time for action – hiding all sprites when the flag is clicked

We're going to animate our card, which means we're going to be changing the default appearances of the sprites in our card. Therefore, we need to think about the starting values of our sprites. As the first step in our animation, we'll hide all sprites so that we start with a blank screen. Then, we can introduce and animate each sprite in turn as shown in the following steps:

1. Select the **Happy Birthday** sprite to display its script area.

2. We'll use the click on the green flag as an event to trigger our script. From the **Events** palette, drag the **when flag clicked** block to the scripts area.

3. From the **Looks** palette, snap the **hide** block to **when flag clicked**.

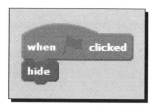

4. Hide each of the letters that spell mom using the same script. Try the following shortcut:

1. Right-click on the Happy Birthday script and select duplicate. The script attaches to your mouse cursor.

2. Drag the script to one of the other sprites in the sprite list and click on it. The script copies to the sprite.

3. Duplicate the script for the remaining sprites, with the exception of the stage.

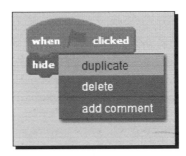

5. Check your work. Click on each sprite and verify whether it has the script that hides the sprite when the green flag is clicked.

6. Click on the green flag and watch our greeting, Happy Birthday, Mom, disappear from the screen.

7. In the current state, you can make the sprites reappear by right-clicking on each sprite in the sprite list and choosing **show**.

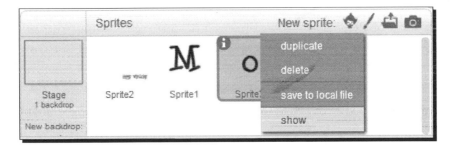

What just happened?

As creative directors, we want control over when and how our sprites enter the stage. For this project, we don't want Happy Birthday, Mom passively sitting there, so we send them backstage.

The **when flag clicked** block, when added to the script area for each sprite, tells each sprite to do something when the green flag is clicked. In our example, we tell them to hide, which clears each sprite from the stage. In the programming context, we're initializing our project. In other words, we're explicitly setting the starting view of our card. This will be common in most of the projects we create. In other examples of initialization, we will sometimes want to hide or show a sprite, position a sprite, or give a variable a specific value when the user starts the project. Clicking on the green flag is one such event that we can use, but any of the other **Event** blocks can be also used to initialize a sprite's starting values.

Time for action – displaying happy birthday

Can you imagine mom's confusion? She clicks on the green flag, and the screen goes blank. That's like going to a play where all the actors are sitting on the stage in front of the curtain until show time. Then, when the curtain goes up, all the actors disappear. However, we don't go to the theater to watch an empty stage. We want actors. Without further fuss, let's introduce our sprites:

1. Let's bring out the Happy Birthday sprite first. Select the **Happy Birthday** sprite from the sprite list.

2. From the **Control** palette, add the **wait (1) secs** block to the existing script to create a bit of delay and to allow the Happy Birthday sprite to display.

3. Before we show the sprite, let's set the default size, adding the **set size to ()** block. I set the size to **300**, but your design may require a different value. The value inside the **set to ()** block is a percentage.

4. Show the sprite by adding the **show** block from the **Looks** palette.

5. Run the script by clicking on the green flag. Happy Birthday disappears and reappears one second later. Now, let's make it pulse.

6. From the **Control** palette, snap the **forever** block in place below the **show** block.

7. From the **Looks** palette, drag the **change size by ()** block into the **forever** block. Change the value on the **change size by ()** block to `-20`.

8. Add a second **change size by ()** block to the `forever` loop and change the size to `20`.

9. From the **Looks** palette, add the **wait () secs** block between the two **change by size ()** blocks and enter a value of `.5` seconds.

10. From the **Events** palette, add a **broadcast** block between the **show** and **forever** blocks.

11. On the **broadcast** block, add a new message: `hi mom`.

12. Click on the green flag to make Happy Birthday pulsate on the screen.

If you haven't already done so, you can stop your pulsating sprite by clicking on the stop button.

What just happened?

Like a beating heart, the "Happy Birthday" text contracts and expands on the stage as long as the script runs. We get the pulsating effect from the blocks of code in the `forever` loop. We increase the size by 20 pixels, and then half a second later, we decrease the size by 20 pixels.

The **set size to (300)** block does something very important. It resets the size of the sprite each time it runs. Otherwise, the size of the sprite will get increasingly smaller as you run and stop the script multiple times because you will stop and start the script while it's in the process of getting bigger or smaller. Let's say you stop the script during the **wait ()** block and after the size was changed by -20 units. Then, when you start the script again, everything starts from the beginning. Now, the **change size by -20** block just ran a second time, but was only negated one time. Scratch remembers state, which makes it necessary to set the size when the green flag is clicked on. That's why we explicitly initialize the sprite's size at 300 percent each time the user runs the project by clicking on the flag. This ensures the sprite always has a correct starting value and helps ensure the user has the correct experience.

Before our sprite enters into its infinite loop, it broadcasts the message **hi mom**. Nothing happened in our script as a result of the broadcast because we have not yet programmed any other sprites to act on the **hi mom** message.

Specifying memorable names and comments

We haven't focused on naming conventions yet, but we just created a new broadcast message with a unique name. So, I'm going to use this opportunity to introduce the importance of naming things in our projects.

If we look closely at our list of sprites, we see the following names: Sprite1, Sprite2, Sprite3, and Sprite4. The broadcast messages would follow an equally bland naming convention. If we allow this default naming convention to continue, we'll easily lose track of our objects in Scratch.

Time for action – renaming sprites

Let's rename our sprites by performing the following steps:

1. Select **Sprite1** from the sprite list and click on the blue i icon to display the sprite properties. Change **Sprite1** to **Happy Birthday**.

2. Rename the remaining sprites with a memorable name, such as **First M**, **Second M**, and **O**.

Each sprite in the list can now be identified by a unique name.

What just happened?

To the computer, **Sprite3** is just as good as **First M**, but humans benefit from associating sprites, costumes, backdrops, lists, variables, and messages to a descriptive name. In our example project, we spell mom from individual sprites. How do we know if Sprite2 is the First M or the last M? But if we rename **Sprite2** to **First M**, we have no doubt.

In addition to providing context, names provide a way for us to easily identify our objects later. For example, if we broadcast one message as message 1 and another as message 2, we may not know which message does what when it's time to make a sprite perform an action based on that message. If the message becomes **hi mom**, then we know that the message signals the beginning of the mom animation.

As meaningful names give us a context and understanding about the object, it helps us and other programmers understand our code later. As you create your projects, don't rely on Scratch's default naming. Change it as necessary.

Inserting comments into our code

A topic closely related to naming our objects is adding comments to our scripts. Adding comments to scripts provides a way for us to explain complicated scripts. Commenting allows us and other programmers to easily understand our code.

Time for action – adding comments to a script

Let's add a quick comment that annotates the broadcast block in the Happy Birthday sprite's script:

1. Select the Happy Birthday script. Right-click somewhere in the scripts area and select **add comment**.

2. In the yellow box that appears, type the following: the "hi mom" broadcast signals the second m sprite to start its animation.

3. Now click on the yellow comment box and drag it to the broadcast (hi mom) block. Then, release the block. This can be tricky, but the goal is to attach the comment to the block. See the following screenshot:

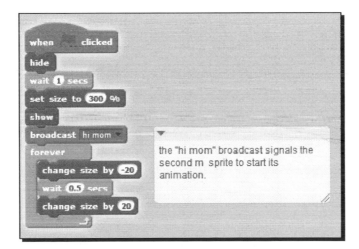

What just happened?

Commenting our code is one of those things that we should always do more often because it helps other people understand our code. And in reality, this can help us understand what we did when we open a project we haven't worked on in months.

Transforming sprites with graphical effects

Scratch provides two blocks in the **Looks** palette to allow us to apply a variety of graphical transformations to our sprites. The effects are color, fisheye, pixelate, mosaic, brightness, ghost, and whirl.

Time for action – transforming sprites

Next, we want to introduce the sprites that spell mom, and as we show the letters, we'll use the **graphical effects** to transform the letters:

1. We're going to start by adding the **when I receive ()** block to the scripts area for **Second M**.

2. To unhide the letter M, we need to add the **show ()** block.

3. Click on the green flag to see the script run so far. As Happy Birthday flashes on the screen, the second letter M appears on the screen. Click on the stop button when you're ready to continue.

4. We're going to transform the m by using the mosaic effect and a repeat loop. From the **Control** palette, snap the **repeat ()** block to the bottom of the **show** block and change the value to 25.

5. From the **Looks** palette, add the **change () effect by ()** block to the **repeat** loop. Change the effect from **color** to **mosaic** by selecting **mosaic** from the drop-down list as seen in the following screenshot:

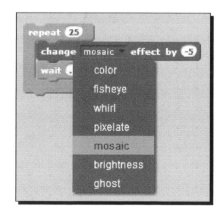

6. Click on the green flag and watch the effect of our action. Our m is a mosaic, but it's no longer readable. Click on stop when you're ready to continue.

7. From the **Looks** palette, double-click on the **clear graphic effects** block to redisplay the letter m. A shortcut to run the block is to click on the block name, which in this case clears any effects.

8. Snap another **repeat ()** block to the bottom of the first **repeat ()** block and set the value to **25**.

9. Insert a second **change () effect by ()** block into the new **repeat 10** block. Change the effect to **mosaic** and set the value to **-25**.

10. If you run this script now, the mosaic happens quickly. You can slow down the effect so that it's visible by adding a **wait () secs** block after each of the **change () effect by ()** blocks. Try a small value, such as **.1**.

11. Next, we need the script to announce when it's finished so we can signal the next letter in the animation. Add a **broadcast ()** block and create a new message named **next m**.

The following screenshot shows the script we've just created:

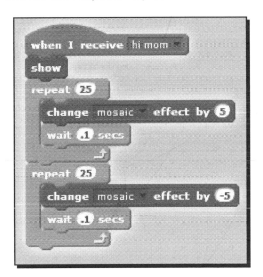

To see what that script does, click on the green flag. The following screenshot shows the change in the letter m as we apply the **change (mosaic) effect by (25)** command:

The following screenshot shows the finished product after we apply the **change (mosaic) effect by (-25)** command:

What just happened?

Finally, we acknowledged the Happy Birthday sprite's **hi mom** broadcast message. Hi mom was the cue that told **Second M** to enter the stage with dramatic effect.

Once the letter "m" displayed, it split apart to form a pattern of its own before it reconstituted itself into a whole letter. The code that created our pattern was straight forward. First, we split the "m" into a mosaic 25 times via the **repeat ()** block, which turned the single letter into 25 smaller copies of itself.

The second **repeat ()** block also ran 25 times, but it changed the mosaic effect by -5 units each time. The second **repeat** block undid the effects of the first **repeat ()** block through negation. This has the practical effect of running the **clear graphical effects** block with a big difference. The **clear graphical effects** block will abruptly turn the sprite back to its original state. By using a second **repeat ()** block to undo each step of the first **repeat ()** block, the animation continues until the sprite returns to normal.

Graphical transformations

We can change the appearance of a sprite very easily, as we have seen with the Happy Birthday card, and Scratch includes several special effects that we can apply directly to the sprite or its costume.

The effects in the following table can be found in the **change () effect by ()** and **set () effect to ()** blocks in the **Looks** palette.

Effect	What it does	Sample usage
color	This effect changes the color of the sprite. A sprite or costume can have up to 200 color effects.	◆ While creating art ◆ To visually signify a different state
fisheye	This effect distorts the sprite by rounding the edge as if you're looking at it through a glass or peep hole.	◆ To distort the sprite ◆ For use as a transition effect
whirl	This effect twists the sprite around a center point and produces an effect similar to throwing a pebble in the water. The greater the whirl effect, the more difficult it is to see.	◆ To distort the sprite ◆ For use as a transition effect ◆ To give a spin
pixelate	This effect increases the size of the pixels in the image so that you can see them. However, it creates a blurry image.	◆ To blur an image ◆ For use as a transition effect ◆ To cover up another sprite
mosaic	This effect splits the sprite into a pattern of smaller images of itself.	◆ For use as a transition effect ◆ To split a single sprite into multiple

Effect	What it does	Sample usage
brightness	This effect increases the luminance of the sprite to make it appear brighter.	◆ To make a sprite glow ◆ To make a sprite dimmer
ghost	This effect makes the sprite transparent so that you can see other sprites and backgrounds through the sprite. A value of 100 hides the sprite by making it completely transparent; -100 shows the sprite.	◆ To hide a sprite ◆ To create a fade in/out effect ◆ To create transparency (like a ghost)

The following screenshot shows all the graphical effects as applied to Gobo:

In the preceding screenshot, the effects on the first row are normal, color, fisheye, and whirl. The effects on the second row are pixelate, mosaic, brightness, and ghost. All the graphical effects can be undone by clicking on the **clear graphic effect** block. You can also undo the effect by negating the original effect. For example, if you set a fisheye effect of 100, you can return to normal by applying a fisheye effect of -100.

Comparing the repeat and forever blocks

Like the **forever** block, the **repeat ()** block creates a loop that runs the blocks inside the loop. The **repeat ()** block differs from the **forever** block in that we specify the count for which the loop will run.

In addition to typing a number in the repeat block, we can insert variables values via reporter blocks. We will introduce variables in *Chapter 6, Making an Arcade Game – Breakout (Part I)*.

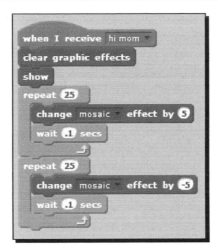

Time for action – turning m in a circle

When we last left our animation, we had the second M displayed on the screen. Now, let's create the script that receives and acts on the next m broadcast message by spinning the First M sprite around in a circle:

1. Add the blocks to show the **First M** sprite when it receives the **next m** broadcast message. If you get stuck, you can take a peek at the screenshot in this exercise.

2. Instead of a graphical effect, we can animate this script with motion by rotating the **First M** sprite. From the **Motion** palette, add the **turn () degrees** block to the show block.

3. Wrap the **turn () degrees** block in a **repeat ()** block. Change the value on the **repeat** block to **36** and set the value on the **turn ()** block to **10**.

4. Check your animation by clicking on the green flag. Note the motion on the **First M** sprite as it spins 360 degrees in a circle.

5. Now that the **First M** sprite is finished with its animation, we need to add a **broadcast ()** block and create a new message named **gimme an O** to signal the letter O.

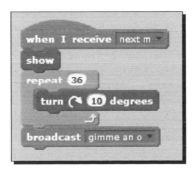

What just happened?

When signaled by the Second M's broadcast message, **First M** tumbled onto the stage. The **repeat ()** block instructed the M to turn 10 degrees clockwise for a total of 36 times. If we multiply 10 degrees by 36, we get 360 degrees, which is otherwise known as a circle.

Have a go hero – cleaning up the animations

Earlier in the chapter, we spoke about initializing our sprites so they always display properly at the start of the project. Go through the sprites we've transformed and ensure they have scripts that reset the sprite to a default starting point. The First M sprite is using motion. Can you add a block to ensure it's always pointing in a position that looks like an M?

Test your work by stopping the project mid-animation and then clicking on the green flag to start it again.

Finally, complete the "mom" animation by showing and animating the letter "o" sprite.

Time for action – making a sprite fade in with the ghost effect

Let's put some finishing touches on our card by adding a butterfly and a personal message to mom:

1. To add a new sprite, click on the **Choose sprite from library** button to open the list of sprites. Browse to **Animals**. Find and select **Butterfly1**. Click on **OK** to add it to the stage.

2. Scratch places the butterfly at the middle of the stage, so we need to drag the butterfly to a place on the stage where it fits into the design.

3. We should add a personal note for mom on her birthday. Use the paint editor and create a new sprite that contains your message. I like to joke with my mom, so for my message, I have typed **Congratulations on your ability to freeze time. I hear you are only 29 again this year**.

4. Resize and reposition the sprites on the stage so that they fit nicely. Take a look at the following screenshot for an example.

5. Right now, the note and the butterfly are not animated, and they remain on the screen for the entire time. We'll change that now by experimenting with a new graphic effect called ghost.

6. Add the **when flag clicked** block to the scripts area for the note and add the **change () effect by ()** block. Change the effect to **ghost**. Set the value to **100**. This effectively hides the sprite.

7. We don't want the note to show up right away, so add a **wait () secs** block with a value of **9 seconds**, and make sure you place it after the **change (ghost) effect by (100)** block.

8. Add a **repeat ()** block and change the value to **20**.

9. Inside the **repeat ()** block, add a **change () effect by ()** block. Change the effect to **mosaic** and set the value to **-5**.

10. As the script is written, the note will fade in very fast. Go ahead and try it by clicking on the green flag.

11. To slow the fade, we can add a **wait () secs** block to the **repeat (20)** block and set a value of **0.2**.

12. Click on the green flag to run the script. Now, our note fades in three seconds after we click on the green flag and after the word mom displays.

13. The script for the note should look like the following screenshot:

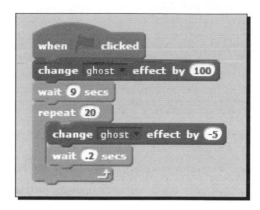

What just happened?

There is often more than one way to accomplish a task, as this exercise illustrates. Setting the ghost effect to 100 is the same as making the sprite invisible or hiding it. So, if you were creating a game where you wanted a sprite to disappear when shot, you could hide it or use the ghost effect to slowly fade out.

In our birthday card example, we repeat the ghost effect by -5 for 20 times. Guess what our ghost value becomes? If we multiply 20 by -5, we get -100, which negates the ghost 100 effect we started with, effectively showing the sprite.

To control the timing of the animation, the .2 second wait at the end of the repeat loop slows down the fade so that we have a gradual transition.

Two ways to control timing

In this chapter, we've used both broadcasts and the **wait ()** block to control the timing of our animations. Let's take a moment to discuss the ramifications of our decisions.

As we have seen in the examples in this chapter, the **broadcast ()** block gives us a way to synchronize events across sprites. For example, when we animated the word mom in our card, we actually brought the second "m" in first, and at the end of the effect, it signaled the first "m" to display. A broadcast can be sent to any sprite within Scratch.

The **wait () secs** block pauses the script for the amount of time specified. However, the **wait () secs** block does not stop other scripts and only interacts with the sprite it's assigned to. It effectively creates a timer or a delay for the script.

Trying to use the **wait () secs** block to synchronize the actions of all our sprites could be a considerable challenge. Could you imagine the revisions we would have to make if we used the **wait () secs** block throughout our animations in this chapter? Every time we alter the animation, we would potentially have to go back through every script to manually set the timing. That's a tedious prospect.

Have a go hero – animating the butterfly

Our birthday card is relatively complete. At the moment, all sprites are animated except the butterfly. Take this opportunity to revise your card or add an animation to the butterfly. Need some ideas? The butterfly has two costumes. Make it fly.

Pop quiz – reviewing the chapter

Q1. Which of the following statements is true about vector and bitmap graphics?

1. Vector graphics are represented by pixels on the screen.
2. Bitmaps use calculations to draw lines.
3. Bitmap images are smooth at any size.
4. Vector graphics are smooth at any size.

Q2. When naming sprites, you should always:

1. Allow Scratch to define the name.
2. Forget about names because they're not important.
3. Pick memorable, meaningful names.
4. Use names based on Greek gods.

Q3. Which of the following best describes a gradient?

1. Gradients fill an area with a solid color.
2. Gradients are only available to vector graphics and transition one color into another color.
3. Gradients are an option in the **change () effect by ()** block that fade two colors together.
4. Gradients gradually blend two colors together and are available in both the vector and bitmap image editor.

Q4. If you want to loop through a set of blocks for an infinite number of times, which block do you use?

1. **forever**

2. **repeat**

3. **broadcast ()**

4. **set () effect by ()**

Q5. Which of the following graphical effects splits a sprite into a pattern of smaller images of itself?

1. **whirl**

2. **pixelate**

3. **mosaic**

4. **brightness**

Q6. How do you copy a script from one sprite to another?

1. Right-click on the script, select **duplicate**, and drag the script to the second sprite.

2. Highlight the script, press *Ctrl + C* to copy it, and press *Ctrl + V* to paste it on the second sprite.

3. Both 1 and 2.

4. You can't copy scripts from one sprite to another.

Summary

We just completed our first Scratch project from concept to completion. In the process, our animated birthday card introduced us to several Scratch programming concepts. We started by using the built-in paint editor to create sprites and explore the differences between bitmap and vector graphics. We then animated these sprites by using graphical transformations. Throughout the chapter we relied on the following blocks to make the animations work: **forever**, **repeat ()**, and **broadcast () and wait () secs**.

In the next chapter, we will create a storybook with multiple scenes. We'll also build navigation that lets the user click through the chapters.

4

Creating a Scratch Story Book

Building on the design and graphic elements we've learned in the previous chapters, we will create a book of barnyard jokes. The project unfolds in a fairly non-linear way, and the scripts are built and tested several blocks at a time, but as we near the end of the chapter, we come to create a seamless transition from the table of contents to a joke and back again. In this chapter, we'll provide a framework that empowers the user to pick their flow through the project.

In addition to practicing our storytelling skills, we will:

- ◆ Design the book's outline
- ◆ Use the **say ()** block to deliver the chapter jokes
- ◆ Play sounds and create sound effects
- ◆ Move sprites based on *x* and *y* coordinates
- ◆ Coordinate scene changes to navigate the book

Designing the outline of a barnyard joke book

Got a good joke or two? Feel free to substitute them for my examples in the following exercise. Our first step is to create a table of contents that users can use to navigate the jokes in our book.

Time for action – designing a clickable table of contents

For our storytelling project, we will create buttons with labels that the user can click to open each joke sequence, which we'll make analogous to a chapter in our Scratch book. We'll refer to these buttons as our table of contents. The steps to design a clickable table of contents are as follows:

1. Open a new project and delete the default Scratch cat sprite.

2. Let's import a button sprite into Scratch. For this project, I'm choosing the **Button2** sprite from the **Things** category because it's a vector image and it has two costumes. Change the sprite name to **Dog TOC** so that we can identify this button as something that appears on our table of contents page.

3. After you import the button into the project, click on the **Costumes** tab to open up the paint editor. We need to add a label.

4. Use the text tool to type Dog in any font you want.

5. Resize the text and position the word **Dog** so that it fits inside the button. Because this is a vector image, we can make the button as big or small as we want.

6. Create a new sprite using the text tool that says Click on a button to open the chapter. Then, name the sprite Instructions.

7. Duplicate the **Dog TOC** sprite and edit the text of the duplicated button to say **Horse** and name the new button Horse TOC. The following screenshot shows our new sprites:

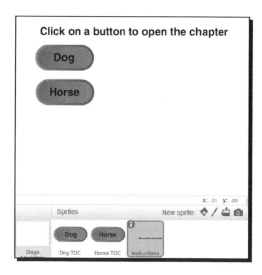

Position the sprites anywhere you like on the screen.

What just happened?

Our book now has a table of contents. You will be able to add to this at a later date, but creating two chapters will be enough to get us started. By using a combination of the sprite library and the image editor, we were able to create a button with a label. As we continue to build the book, we'll make the buttons clickable.

Time for action – adding pages to the book

Next, we are going to add two background images from the Scratch **Backdrop Library** to our project to represent pages in our book.

We'll adapt our backdrops by combining them with a sprite to create something unique for our project. Our objective is to create a single image from a backdrop and a sprite. I'll explain the nuances of this task after we complete the exercise rather than try to explain the reasons as we go.

With the stage selected, let's get started:

1. Use the **Choose backdrop from library** button on the **Backdrops** tab to import **bedroom1** from the **Indoors** category and **hay field** from the **Outdoors** category.

2. From the **Backdrops** tab, select **hay field** to open it in the paint editor. Convert the image to vector format, or you'll have unsatisfactory results when we import the microphone in the following steps.

3. Next, we're going to import a microphone into the project that we'll use as a visual aid for our scenes. Choose the **Microphone Stand** from the **Things** category in the **Sprite Library**. After you import the microphone as a sprite, open the **Backdrops** tab for the stage and select **hay field**.

4. From the list of sprites (beneath the stage), click and drag the **Microphone** sprite into the **hay field** backdrop in the paint editor. This places the sprite into the backdrop as seen in the next screenshot.

5. We can position and resize the microphone object in the paint editor by clicking on it with the **select** tool and dragging it around the image. For our purposes, position it in the bottom-right of the stage. The following screenshot shows the status of our project so far. Notice that our stage displays two microphone stands. One is a sprite and the other is part of the backdrop. We'll fix this in due time, but let's pause to review our exercise first.

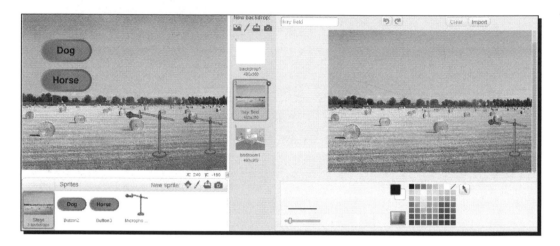

What just happened?

The backdrops we added begin to provide some graphical context to our story. For example, many pet dogs like to spend their days inside on a bed, and while we may not find horses roaming the hay fields, they do eat hay. It's up to us to use design effectively in our stories. We're also able to suspend our disbelief as we create our story. It does not matter if you put your horse on the moon or your dog in an aquarium.

The microphone adds a layer to the story. This is a joke book, and the microphone is a perfect way for our characters to deliver the joke.

In addition to the design, we also discovered a technical feature of Scratch. Scratch 2.0 convolutes the process of combining sprites into a single image, but as the example demonstrated, it's possible to combine them. Combining sprites with backdrops allows us to further customize the sprites and backdrops included with Scratch.

If you didn't follow the instructions closely and left the **hay field** backdrop as a bitmap image, you will have noticed a white box around your microphone when you added it to the backdrop. Undoing the change and converting the backdrop to vector format before you add the microphone will get a seamless image.

Now our **hay field** backdrop consists of two objects: the original backdrop and the microphone stand. We'll be able to edit those objects independently if we edit the backdrop, but when the backdrop image displays on the Scratch stage, it will appear as one image.

For this project, I made a design decision to integrate the two images because it will create one less sprite in my list and will be one less sprite that we have to manipulate as we transition our chapters. This decision has a tradeoff. We will not be able to independently add scripts to the microphone in our project because we made it part of the backdrop.

Time for action – adding a sprite to the Backpack

Right now, our project still displays the extra microphone sprite we imported. That was a necessary step so that we could combine the sprite with the backdrop; however, it's cluttering our project. And because we will want to use this same microphone throughout our chapters, we don't want to have to re-import the microphone each time. We'll declutter our project by using Scratch's Backpack. The **Backpack** is a feature in the online project editor for users who are signed in. If you're not signed in to the online project editor, the Backpack will not be available.

Let's work through the steps, and then we'll explain:

1. The **Backpack** is collapsed (that is, closed) at the bottom-right of the Scratch interface. You can open it by clicking on the up triangle next to the word **Backpack**.

2. Drag the **Microphone Stand** sprite into the open **Backpack** to create a copy.

3. Now, you can delete the **Microphone Stand** sprite from the sprites list by right-clicking on the sprite thumbnail in the sprites list and choosing **Delete**.

4. Now let's see how we can add the microphone to the bedroom backdrop. Open the **bedroom1** backdrop in the **Backdrops** tab so that it displays in the paint editor.

5. From the **Backpack**, drag the microphone onto the **bedroom1** backdrop in the paint editor.

6. Resize and position the microphone object as needed.

7. The following screenshot shows the microphone in the **Backpack** and the sprite added to the backdrop:

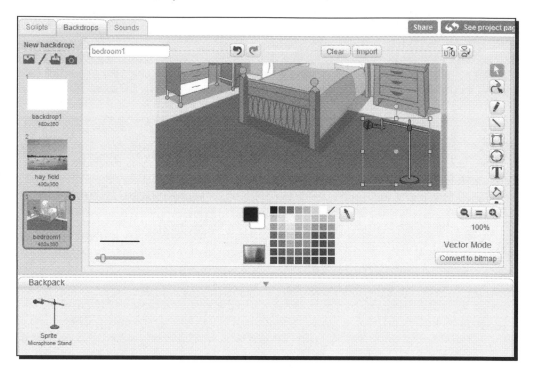

What just happened?

Welcome to the **Backpack**—a new feature in Scratch 2.0. We're making a creative but modest use of the feature in the context of this project as a way to combine the microphone with any backdrop that we add in the future.

The benefit we get from removing the unused sprite is that our sprite list stays cleaner and we don't have to worry about inadvertently showing the **Microphone Stand** sprite when it shouldn't be shown. In other words, we limit our ability to make future mistakes.

Using the Backpack to store sprites and scripts

As our project example demonstrates, the **Backpack** can hold things, but it's capable of holding more than just a sprite.

When you drag a sprite to the **Backpack**, it will copy the sprite, its costumes, and all of the scripts associated with the sprite. In addition, you could drag an individual script to the **Backpack**.

The **Backpack** is only available online and to users who sign-in to Scratch.

And like a backpack on a second-grader, the contents of the Scratch **Backpack** follow the user from one project to the next. So, the sprites and scripts we add to the Backpack will now will be available to all of the projects we create, edit, or remix, making the **Backpack** our portable collection of our favorite things.

If we create a script that you think may be useful in the future, feel free to add it to your **Backpack**.

Building a joke with say blocks and sounds

Now that we have the basic page designs defined via our backdrops, let's add in a horse as our character for the hay field scene and write some lines for its comedy routine.

Time for action – making a horse talk with the say block

Right now, we have the **Dog TOC** and **Horse TOC** sprites displayed on the screen. Go ahead and hide them from the stage by right-clicking on the sprites and selecting hide. Then, make sure the hay field displays on the stage by clicking on the **hay field** backdrop from your list of stage backgrounds:

1. Import the **horse1** sprite from the **Animals** category of Scratch's **Sprite Library**.

2. Position the horse next to the microphone by dragging the sprite on the stage with your mouse. If the horse and microphone seem out of proportion, resize the horse sprite using the shrink or grow tools.

3. Next, we'll try our hand at joke writing. Click on the **Scripts** tab to get started.

4. From the **Looks** palette, drag the **say () for ()** block into the script area. Change the message from **Hello!** to How do you make it rain?. Change the time value to **4**.

5. If the sprite is close to the edge of the stage, the speech bubble that displays from the **say** block may appear at the backend of the sprite. If this happens, move the sprite away from the edge.

6. Add a **say () for ()** block. Change the message to Mow a hay field, and change the time from **2** seconds to **3**. I didn't say we were going to write good jokes; check with your local farmer to understand the relationship of hay making to rain. In all sincerity, you can write any joke you want.

7. Add a **wait () secs** block. Change the time from **1** to **3** seconds.

8. Add the **say () for ()** block to the script. Change the message to `Hello, is this thing on?`.

9. Double-click on the script to watch our horse tell its first joke.

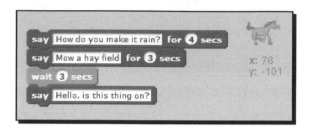

What just happened?

We wrote a short script to deliver the joke using the **say () for ()** blocks to display speech bubbles, and after three seconds of silence, our horse tossed out a comedic cliché, "Is this thing on?"

We used two variations of the **say** block. For the joke and punchline, the horse speaks for a specified number of seconds. However, at the end of the script, the **say** block we added did not specify a time value. And if you look at the stage, you'll see that the speech bubble still displays **Hello, is this thing on?**. We're going to use that say block to our advantage in the next exercise.

Time for action – synchronizing and animating the horse

The first part of this exercise will be familiar to you. We want to animate the horse using its costumes. However, we'll combine that animation with another say block to create a fluid scene:

1. Continue building the script by adding a **next costume** block.

2. Add a **wait () secs** block.

3. Add a **next costume** block. Note that since we are not actually going to call the name of the costume for the **horse1** sprite, we're not going to take the time to rename them from their defaults.

4. Add a **say ()** block with an empty input value.

5. Double-click on the script to run the code.

What just happened?

It was a tough crowd, and the joke fell flat, causing the horse to nervously rear up on its hind legs and say **Hello, Is this thing on?**. Even though our script technically runs the **say (Hello, Is this thing on?)** block before switching to the costume of the horse on its hind legs via the **next costume** block, any delay between the two actions is going to be difficult to notice, which is the intentional effect; we want those two actions to happen in a fluid way.

By adding a **say ()** block at the end of the script with an empty value, we clear the speech bubble. The difference in the two say blocks warrants some discussion.

When we use a **say () for () secs** block, the speech bubble displays on the stage for the amount of time specified, and more importantly, the script stops when the specified time elapses. If we use the **say ()** block with no time value, the speech bubble displays and the script continues, meaning we can animate the sprite while the speech bubble displays as we demonstrated in our script.

Speech bubbles enable us to convey a conversation; however, the text can only be displayed on the screen. While it would be cool to have a computer-generated voice read the value of the say block, that's not yet possible in Scratch. Maybe we can ask the Scratch Team for a feature enhancement.

For our next exercise, we're going to add some prerecorded sounds from Scratch's library.

Time for action – importing a horse sound

Let's add some further context to our story by incorporating some actual sounds. As we'll see in the exercise, Scratch includes a horse sound, making it relatively easy to create some thematic stories based on the included media:

1. With the horse sprite selected, click on the **Sounds** tab.
2. Click on the **Choose sound from library** button to display Scratch's sound library.

3. Browse to the **Animal** category and select **Horse**.

4. To demo a sound before you import it, click on the play button next to each sound.

5. Click on **OK** to add the sound to the list of sounds for the horse sprite. To listen to the horse whinnying, click on the play button in the sound editor.

6. Duplicate the **horse** sound by right-clicking on the sound and selecting **Duplicate**.

7. Select all of **horse2** in the sound editor and apply the **softer** effect. To select the sound wave, click on the left-hand side of the sound editor and drag your mouse to the left. This is the same selection technique we used to highlight text in a document.

8. Let's give **horse2** a better name. Change the name to **horse softer** to correspond to the effect we used. You can change the name of the selected sound above the sound editor.

9. Now let's add the sound to several places in our script. From the **Sound** palette, add the **play sound until done** block to the top of the script and select the **horse** sound.

10. Insert a second **play sound () until done** block after the **say (Mow a hay field) for (1) secs** block. Select **horse softer** as the sound to play.

11. Insert the **play sound ()** block after the **next costume** and before the **wait (1) secs** block. Select **horse** as the sound to play.

12. The following screenshot shows our script so far:

What just happened?

We used Scratch's sound library to add a horse sound to the scene as we continued to build our story. We introduced the horse with a whinny, and then we reiterated the sound after the joke's punchline.

By duplicating the whinny and applying the softer effect, we created a timid horse. Right about then, the horse is realizing that if he has to explain the joke, it's not a good joke.

At the end of the script, we used the plain **play () sound** block to play the **horse** sound while the script continues to run. This allowed the horse to do several things at one time: say **Hello, Is this thing on?**, rear up, and whinny. This combination at the end enabled us to reinforce the nervous horse idea.

Playing supported sound formats

Scratch includes a library of sounds that you can use in any of your projects, and you can also easily import your own sounds. The **Upload sound from file** button on the **Sound** tab provides a dialog box that lets you select sounds on your own computer.

In addition to the MP3 format, Scratch can play uncompressed WAV, AU, and AIF sound files.

Positioning a sprite by its coordinates

With our horse scene complete, we'll move on to the dog. Our dog is also a comedian, but in this scene, we're going to be moving the dog across the stage. Therefore, we'll have to position the sprite to be exactly where we need it to be in order for the scene to play out.

Time for action – moving the dog based on x and y coordinates

In this exercise, we're going to use the *x* and *y* coordinates to move our dog:

1. Let's prepare the stage by hiding the **horse1** sprite by right-clicking on the thumbnail in the sprites list and choosing **Hide**. Then, display the **bedroom1** backdrop on the stage.

2. Next, add the **dog2** sprite from the **Animals** category of Scratch's sprite library.

3. Position the dog so that it's talking into the microphone. Resize the sprite as necessary.

4. With the dog in position, let's find the *x* and *y* coordinates of the sprite so we can ensure the dog always returns to this position. Select the **dog2** sprite in the sprite list and then click on the **i** icon on the sprite thumbnail to display the sprite properties pane as seen in the following screenshot:

5. Now, we'll create the script that always returns the dog to the spot in front of the microphone. From the **Motion** palette, drag the **set x to ()** block to the scripts area. Change the value to the dog's *x* value. My example uses **22**.

6. Add the **set y to ()** block. Change the value to the dog's *y* value. My example uses **-88**.

7. Let's identify some coordinates on the left-hand side of the stage by the desk because we will want our dog to move there after it's done telling the joke. As you move your mouse around the stage, Scratch tracks the *x* and *y* position of the mouse. The information displays the **x:** and **y:** values in the space between the stage and the **New sprite** icons as seen in the following screenshot:

8. From the **Motion** palette, add the **glide () secs to x: () y: ()** block to the scripts area, but do not attach it to the **set x: (22)** and **set y: (-88)** blocks.

9. The **glide () secs to x: () y: ()** block is populated with the current **x** and **y** coordinates of the selected sprite. Let's change the coordinates to where we want the dog to go. Change the **x** value to -138 and the **y** value to -2. Change the **secs** value to **2**.

 The more seconds you add to the glide block, the longer it takes the dog to reach its coordinates.

10. Run each script by clicking on each stack and observe how the dog changes positions. The following screenshots show the scripts so far:

11. The following screenshot shows the result of the glide block by positioning the dog next to the bed and in front of the desk:

What just happened?

We issued a series of commands and our dog responded with precision. The first script sets the dog's X and Y coordinates next to the microphone. The second script moves the dog to the new X and Y coordinates in front of the desk by gliding to the point over the course of two seconds. If we wanted the dog to amble along, we could set the value to a higher value, such as 10 seconds.

When we built the horse scene, we didn't need to know the position of the horse because it didn't move. Each time we displayed the horse, it was in the same location.

However, the dog will change position as the scene plays out, and since Scratch remembers the sprite's previous position, we need to ensure that the dog always starts in front of the microphone when the scene starts.

Did you notice that the dog walked backwards when you ran the **glide** block? Of course you did. We'll fix that up in due time.

Locating sprites with x and y coordinates

Scratch uses the **Cartesian coordinate system** to define the positions on the stage. If you're not familiar with the Cartesian coordinate system, it's basically a set of two points (numbers) that describe a location. There are a lot of everyday items that are located by describing them in terms of two points. For example, a street address is generally described in terms of a street name and a number, as in 352 Main Street. In another example, spreadsheets are comprised of cells that are located by a lettered column and a numbered row. Here, B2 represents the cell in the second column, second row of the spreadsheet. Cartesian coordinates are represented in terms of *x* and *y* positions, as our previous example demonstrated.

The *x* axis divides the stage into equal halves horizontally, and the *y* axis divides the stage into equal halves vertically. The two axes intersect in the middle of the screen or at coordinates 0,0 to form four equal quadrants, or blocks.

If a sprite has a positive *x* value, it's positioned in the right half of the stage. If a sprite has a positive *y* value, it's positioned in the top half of the stage. A negative *x* value can be found in the left half of the stage, and a negative *y* value can be found in the bottom half of the stage.

The following screenshot shows the Scratch stage with an *x* and *y* grid as a background. The background displays the four equal quadrants with key points labeled. This grid is one of Scratch's included backdrops and provides a very nice graphical representation of the coordinate system.

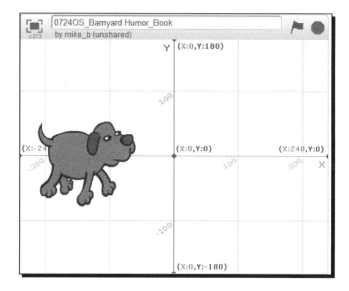

When we locate a sprite on the stage by the coordinates, Scratch uses the center point of the sprite to determine exactly where the sprite is placed. We'll explore the sprite's center in more detail in *Chapter 6, Making an Arcade Game – Breakout (Part I)*.

The following table defines several key coordinates on the stage. The coordinates are listed in the format (*x*, *y*).

Coordinates (*x*, *y*)	Location
(0,0)	This marks the center point of the stage.
(240, 0)	The x=240 identifies the right edge of the stage. The y=0 represents the vertical midpoint on the right edge of the stage.
(-240, 0)	The x=-240 identifies the right edge of the stage. The y=0 represents the vertical midpoint on the right edge of the stage.

Coordinates (x, y)	Location
(0, 180)	The y=180 identifies the top edge of the stage. The x=0 represents the horizontal midpoint on the top edge of the stage.
(0, -180)	The y=-180 identifies the bottom edge of the stage. The x=0 represents the horizontal midpoint on the bottom edge of the stage.

Creating a new costume

Most dogs don't walk across the room backwards like ours does. Let's get our dog walking forward by creating a new costume that points in the direction we want to go.

Time for action – duplicating, flipping, and switching a sprite's costume

We've established throughout our exercises in this book that sprites have costumes, and we've chosen sprites that have more than one costume because it's been convenient to our projects. We can, however, add costumes to a sprite. In this exercise, we'll add a costume by duplicating an existing costume as follows:

1. With the dog sprite selected, click on the **Costumes** tab.

2. Right-click on the **dog2-b** costume and select **duplicate** to create a fourth costume called **dog2-b2**.

3. Select the **dog2-b2** costume and then click on the **flip left-right** button at the top of the image editor. The costume **dog2-b2** now faces to the left.

4. Name the costume **face left**. Also, change the name of **dog2-a** to **face right**. See the following screenshot:

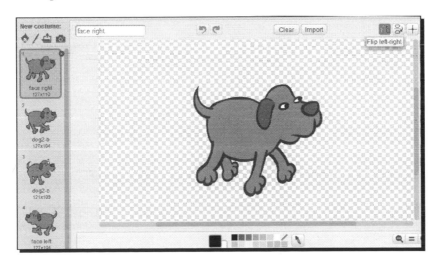

5. To use the new sprite, add the **switch costume to ()** block to the top of the glide block. Select the **face left** costume.

6. Add another **switch costume to ()** block to the top of the script that starts with the **set x to (22)** block. Select **face right** as the costume.

7. Click on each script to run the blocks of code.

What just happened?

Costumes change the appearance of the sprite, and in this case, duplicating a costume and flipping it horizontally points the dog in the opposite direction. We used the **switch costume to (face-left)** block to display the left-facing costume before we glide. When we position the dog in front of the microphone, we use another **switch costume to** block to position the dog correctly.

Comparing costumes to sprites

We'll use the following definition from the Scratch Wiki to describe a sprite. **Sprites** are the *objects* that perform actions in a project. While the stage can also be programmed in a project, most projects have at least one sprite as well because only sprites can move. We can think of the "actions" as a reference to the scripts, costumes, and other properties that we assign to a sprite. I generally will not refer to sprites as objects because *sprites* is a more specific word; however, it's worth mentioning sprites as objects because other people, particularly people from a computer science background may tend to think in terms of objects.

We use a costume to manipulate the appearance of the sprite by switching between the costumes. Another way to think about costumes would be as *frames*, as in the frames of an animation. By using costumes, we can easily make a sprite run, walk, dance, or explode into pixels. In our previous exercise, we switched to a costume to point our dog in the direction we wanted to make it walk. There could be other ways to script this behavior, but the switching costume approach accomplishes the goal simply.

In our exercise, we duplicated an existing sprite's costume, but you can also add a costume by drawing it or by importing a costume from Scratch's library (at the top of the **Costumes** tab). When working in a Scratch project, it's possible to import a sprite with costumes or just one costume.

The Scratch Library has the benefit of including many sprites that are packaged with multiple costumes that provide a great way to jump-start our animations. When you choose a sprite from the library, you can tell if the sprite has costumes by clicking on its thumbnail. The number of costumes will display below the sprite costume. The **Breakdancer1** sprite, as seen in the following screenshot, includes three costumes that will be imported with the sprite:

If you're working from the Costumes pane and want to import a single costume into the sprite you're editing, then you **Choose costume from library** from the **New costume** icons. The difference between choosing the costume versus choosing the sprite is that choosing a costume shows all the individual costumes of sprite for selection. The following screenshot shows the three costumes that are available to the **Breakdancer1** sprite when you use the **Choose costume from library** option in the **Costumes** tab:

Composing custom sound effects

Earlier in the chapter, we used the **play sound ()** block. Scratch includes several sound-related blocks, such as the **play (drum)** block, that allow us to create music and sound effects for use in our projects.

Time for action – creating drum sound effects

Let's try our hand at creating a drum effect that plays on the punchline of the dog's joke. We'll create the dog's joke in the next *Have a go hero* exercise:

1. From the **Sound** palette, drag the **set tempo to () bpm** block to the script area, but do not attach it to an existing stack of blocks. Change the **bpm** value to **150**.

2. From the **Sound** palette, add a **play drum () for () beats** block. Use the block's default value (a snare drum for **.25** beats).

3. Snap the **rest for () beats** block from the **Sound** palette to the script and change the value to **.4**.

4. Add two more **play drum () for () beats** blocks, leaving the drum value set to one. Change the beats value to **.1** for both.

5. Add another **play drum () for () beats** block to the end of the script and change the drum value to **4 (Crash Cymbals)**. Set the beats value to **.5**.

6. Click on the stack of blocks to listen to the effect.

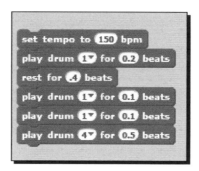

Feel free to tweak the values and experiment with the sound.

What just happened?

By arranging three blocks to affect the drum effects, tempo, and rest, we created a familiar *da dat dat chsh* drum roll. If we wanted a faster pace, we could set a higher beats per minute (bpm) value in the **set tempo to () bpm** block. We're going to use this sound effect to punctuate the punchline of the dog's joke, which we haven't written yet.

Creating sound effects and music

In the **Sounds** palette, Scratch provides several blocks that can be used to create sound effects (as we did) or to create your own musical scores. The following table lists the sound blocks that will help you create your own music and sound effects:

Block	Description
play drum() for () beats	Select from a variety of percussion instruments, including drums, cymbals, triangles, cowbells, and hand claps. You can also set the number of beats the drum plays for.
play note () for () beats	Specify both the note to play and the beat. Notes are annotated with numbers in a range of 0 to 127, and the pitch gets higher as the number increases. A list of predefined numbers and notes are available in the note drop-down list, including the following key notes:
	48 – low C
	60 – middle C
	72 – high C
set instrument to ()	Use in conjunction with the play note block to set the instrument for the note. The current instrument values are between 1 and 21 and include a variety of options including drums, organs, and flutes.
rest for () beats	The block plays silence for the specified number of beats. The default value is .25.
set tempo to () bpm	Specify the beats per minute (bpm) that the note or drum plays. The higher the bpm, the faster the tempo.
change tempo by ()	Increase or decrease the tempo by the specified amount. Use a negative number to decrease the tempo.
set volume to ()	The default volume is 100 percent, but you can limit the volume with this block. The **change volume by** block can also be used to increase or decrease the volume.

Have a go hero – writing a joke sequence for the dog

You should be able to build the joke sequence for the dog without much help from me. Feel free to incorporate your own joke, but I'm going to use a top three list, as in "What are the top three reasons dogs don't use computers?" The responses will be:

◆ It's hard to read the monitor with your head cocked to one side.

◆ They can't stop hunting the mouse.

◆ CarPAW Tunnel Syndrome!

In the next exercise, we'll refer to this block of code as the joke sequence.

Time for action – integrating the dog's joke sequence

With jokes in hand, let's integrate them into our scene:

1. Snap the joke sequence to the script that ends with the **set y to ()** block. In the next screenshot, my joke sequence is everything between the **say (What are the top three reasons dogs don't use computers?) for (4) secs** and **say (CarPAW Tunnel Syndrome!) for (3) secs** blocks.

2. Add the stack that ends with the **glide (1) secs to x: (-138) y: (2)** block to the end of the joke sequence. Check your work against the following screenshot:

3. Now let's add our drum effect to the script. We have three jokes; therefore, we will use a **broadcast () and wait** block to play the drum effect after each line. After each joke, insert a **broadcast and wait** block. Create a new broadcast message named **play drums** and select the **play drums** message in each **broadcast () and wait** block.

4. Add a **when I receive ()** block to the top of the drum effects stack and select the **play drums** message.

5. Double-click on the stack that contains the joke sequence to watch the scene unfold.

```
when I receive  play drums ▼         switch costume to  dog2-a ▼
set tempo to  150  bpm               set x to  22
play drum  1▼  for  0.2  beats       set y to  -88
rest for  .4  beats                  say  What are the top 3 reasons dogs don't use computers?  for  4  secs
play drum  1▼  for  0.1  beats       wait  1  secs
play drum  1▼  for  0.1  beats       say  It's hard to read the monitor with your head cocked to one side.  for  4  secs
play drum  4▼  for  0.5  beats       broadcast  play drums ▼  and wait
                                     wait  1  secs
                                     say  They can't stop hunting the mouse.  for  4  secs
                                     broadcast  play drums ▼  and wait
                                     wait  1  secs
                                     say  And the number one reason....  for  2  secs
                                     say  Carpal paw syndrome  for  3  secs
                                     broadcast  play drums ▼  and wait
                                     switch costume to  dog2-b2 ▼
                                     glide  1  secs to x:  -138  y:  2
```

x: -138
y: 2

What just happened?

We took our disparate stacks of code and combined them into two stacks that execute our scene. The **broadcast () and wait** block is significant to the timing of our scene. The **broadcast (play drums) and wait** block pauses the script until all the code in all of the **when I receive (play drums)** blocks run. The **broadcast ()** block by comparison will send the broadcast message and continue running the blocks in the remainder of the stack regardless of whether or not the code attached to the **when I receive ()** block completes or not.

After we complete our work in *Chapter 7, Programming a Challenging Gameplay – Breakout (Part II)*, you'll recognize that we could also use custom blocks, which is a new Scratch 2.0 feature to create procedures. In our script, one way would be as good as the other.

Have a go hero – adding context to the dog's scene

We have an opportunity to customize the dog's behavior extensively. Here are a couple of suggestions. Can you make the dog lie on its back on the bed? As another example, one of the dog's costumes has a raised eyebrow, which might be a good expression to show after each line of the joke. I'm sure you can come up with some ways to add meaning to the scene.

Navigating the story and coordinating scenes

With the majority of the project complete, the only steps left are to add some controls to the project so our readers can click from one scene to the next.

Time for action – hiding the table of contents

For navigation, we want to give users the ability to click on an item from the table of contents to play the scene. The user can then click back to the table of contents by clicking on a home link.

1. Let's get back to the plain white background that represents our table of contents. Hide the **Dog2** sprite. With the stage selected, click on the **Backdrops** tab. Select the blank white backdrop.

2. Display the **Dog TOC**, **Horse TOC**, and **Instructions** sprites by right-clicking on each one from the sprites list and selecting **show**.

3. We're going to make the **Dog TOC** sprite clickable, so select the **Dog TOC** from the sprites list.

4. From the **Events** palette, drag the **when this sprite clicked** block into the scripts area. Add a **broadcast ()** block to the script and create a new broadcast message, **hide toc**, because clicking on the **Dog TOC** button will cause the dog scene to load and all visible sprites on the table of content page to hide.

5. Next, add a **hide** block to the script.

6. The script can be seen in the following screenshot:

7. In addition to hiding the clicked button, we want to use the **hide toc** broadcast message as a signal to hide all the visible sprites. Let's start with the **Horse TOC** button. Add the **when I receive ()** block to the **Horse TOC** sprite's script area. Select the **hide toc** message.

8. Add the **hide** block to the **when I receive (hide toc)** block. The following screenshot shows the two block stack:

9. Now we can copy the **when I receive (hide toc)** script to the **Instructions** sprite.

What just happened?

Before we can play our scene, we need to clear the stage in preparation for the dog scene. We use the **broadcast ()** and **when I receive ()** blocks to coordinate what happens when we click on the **Dog TOC** button. Now when we click on the **Dog** button, all the sprites should hide.

Let's reflect on the sprite names in our project so far. There can ultimately be no wrong answers when it comes to naming conventions and vernaculars, and I'm not intent on enforcing any one on you. I think it's a good idea to choose names that provide meaning to you.

Let's break down our current **Dog TOC** example. We can tell by looking at the sprite that it's a button and the **Dog** label gives us a clue as to what scene will load. **TOC** represents the table of contents, which is where the button displays. When we click on the **Dog TOC** sprite, we need to hide the table of contents, which we do with the **hide toc** broadcast. You might notice that the name of our dog character is still the Scratch default **Dog2**. This will drive some of you nuts, but from a practical standpoint, **Dog2** already adequately describes the sprite. Changing the name to Dog, for example, will not add clarity to anything, especially because we're not adding more than one dog sprite to the project.

Time for action – displaying the dog scene

We continue to build around the broadcast message **enter dog** to display the sprites and background of the dog chapter:

1. Now that we have cleared the table of contents, we need to load the dog scene. We'll bring in the backdrop first and the dog second. Select the **Dog TOC** sprite.

2. From the **Looks** palette, add the **switch to backdrop to ()** block to the end of the **when this sprite clicked** stack and choose **bedroom1**. The revised script can be seen in the following screenshot:

3. Now let's display the dog. Select the **Dog2** sprite.

4. From the **Events** palette, add the **when backdrop switches to ()** block to the scripts area. Select the **bedroom1** backdrop.

5. From the **Looks** palette, snap the **show** block to the script.

6. Now attach the **when backdrop switches to (bedroom1)** stack to the top of the script that begins with the **switch costume to (facing-right)** stack that initiates the dog's joke sequence.

7. After the scene changes, we want to delay the start of the action for a few seconds so our users have a chance to acclimatize to the switch. Add a **wait () secs** block in place after the **set y to ()** block and change the value to **5**. The revised script can be seen in the following screenshot:

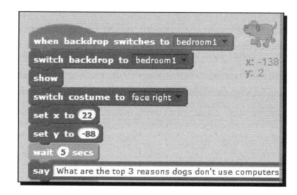

8. Click on the dog button from the table of contents and watch the dog chapter load and play.

What just happened?

With one mouse click, we loaded our wise-cracking dog and learned why dogs don't use computers. Did you notice the sequence? First, we switched the backdrop. Then, we used the backdrop as the cue to display the dog.

We needed to add some timing to control the scene by delaying the start of the joke by five seconds. Without the delay, everything happened at once: the background displayed, the dog displayed, and the joke started. It would have been too abrupt.

Coordinating scenes by backdrop name

In our chapter exercises, we've seen two ways to coordinate the flow of our program. The **broadcast (play drums) and wait** block initiates the drum effects, and the **broadcast (hide toc)** block hides everything on the table of contents. But then we added a new wrinkle by using the **when backdrop switches to ()** block, which is a new Scratch 2.0 block.

The **Dog2** sprite is checking to see if the current backdrop is **bedroom1**, and if the backdrop is **bedroom1**, then the dog's joke sequence plays out. Otherwise, the dog stays hidden and is silent. The **when backdrop switches to ()** block only checks stage backdrops as the name of the block implies.

Time for action – navigating back to the table of contents

After a scene plays out, we need to give our users a way to play the next scene. We'll do that by adding a home button on the scene. We're going to return to the table of contents and allow the user to select the next item. Let's add the controls:

1. The Scratch sprite library includes several buttons we can use. For this exercise, I'm going to import **Button3**. You can use or create any button you like. Just add a text label that says **Home** via the paint editor and give the sprite a name, such as **home button**. Position the **Home** button on the top-left of the stage.

2. From the **Events** palette, drag the **when this sprite clicked** block into the scripts area.

3. Add a **broadcast ()** block to the script and create a new message: **Show TOC**.

4. Add the **hide** block.

5. After we send the message to show the table of contents via the **show TOC** broadcast and hide the **Home** button, we need to switch the backdrop to the first stage backdrop. Add the **switch backdrop to (backdrop1)** block.

6. Now we need to create the script that shows the **Home** button. Add the **when I receive (hide toc)** block to the home sprite to take advantage of a broadcast message we created earlier to hide the table of contents.

7. Add a **show** block. Our two scripts can be seen in the following screenshot:

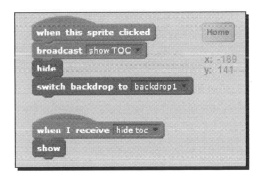

What just happened?

Now we have a way to navigate back to the table of contents for our joke book, and a key part of that navigation are the **show TOC** and **hide toc** broadcast messages. Our script establishes the table of contents page as home; therefore, when we broadcast the **show TOC** message, we're displaying the table of contents (or home). When the user is viewing the home screen, the user doesn't need a way to navigate to home, so we hide the sprite. Then, when we broadcast the **hide toc** message, it means we're loading a scene, and therefore need to show the **Home** button.

Whether we guide the user through the project or make it interactive, we need to think about "what happens when". The answer to the "what happens when" question becomes the basis of how we move our users through the project.

Have a go hero – finishing the sequence and initializing the project

Right now, we're able to switch back and forth from the table of contents to the dog's scene. Take a moment to make the horse scene load when you click on the **Horse TOC** button.

Then, take the necessary steps to initialize the start of the project with the **when flag clicked** block from the **Events** palette to ensure that the project always starts with the table of contents showing.

Pop quiz – checking chapter concepts

Q1. Which of the following best describes the Backpack?

1. It stores revisions of your scripts that can be restored later.

2. It stores scripts and sprites that can be copied among projects.

3. It lists all your created Scratch projects.

4. It contains help files.

Q2. How can we use the **when backdrop switches to ()** block?

1. As an event that runs the script if the selected backdrop displays.

2. To halt all running scripts.

3. To initialize the project's starting values.

4. To coordinate events via a broadcast message.

Q3. If you want to position a sprite in your script, how can you do that?

1. Measure the distance from the edge of the stage.

2. Drag the sprite around to the point on the stage where you want it.

3. Add the glide block to the script.

4. Determine the X and Y coordinates for use in motion blocks, such as the **glide () secs to x: () y: ()** block.

Q4. Which of the following best describes the **play sound () until done** block?

1. The selected sound plays while the scripts continue to run.

2. The selected sound sends a broadcast message.

3. The selected sound plays, and the script does not run the next block in the stack until the sound finishes.

4. The block allows you to select from several drums.

Summary

Sometimes, programming in Scratch can seem like the easy part of creating a project, especially when we have to simultaneously create the storyline and coordinate all the elements to make the story unfold. Fortunately for us, everything gets easier with practice.

We started our work at the beginning of the chapter with the idea to create a book of jokes—and I'll forgive you if you think my jokes are bad—and by the time we finished our exercises, we had a project that could seamlessly navigate through the stories based on the users' selected path. In the process of telling a story via our Scratch book, we got our first good look at using coordinates to precisely locate sprites, explored sound, and coordinated action based on a background.

In the next chapter, we're going to continue our work with backgrounds by creating a slideshow from some of our personal images. We'll explore some of the advanced features of some of the concepts we introduced in this chapter, including hiding the slideshow navigation based on the mouse location and playing back our recorded slide navigation.

5

Creating a Multimedia Slideshow

If you're like me, you have thousands of photos on your computer hard drive. It's time to dust off a few of these photos for our next project as we will be creating a slideshow with images we import from our computers. To help us personalize our slideshow, we'll incorporate generic sounds and custom recordings into our project.

In this chapter, we will do the following:

- Import personal photos as backdrops
- Work with and resize images for use in our projects
- Add slideshow controls to display images
- Play and record sounds
- Locate the *x* and *y* coordinates to locate the mouse and hide the navigation controls
- Display a project in presentation mode

We will start simple with this project and add advanced features as we near the end of the chapter, but the basic slideshow framework should be well within reach of the youngest Scratchers.

Importing photos as backdrops

Before we begin, you might want to look through your photo library. As a backyard beekeeper, I'll be using some of my bee photos. As you look for your own photos, you might want to consider selecting a group of images from a party, a trip, or some other event to help create a theme for the slideshow. A minimum of three photos would be a good place to start as we work through the chapter.

Time for action – importing photos from files

Let's import a batch of photos from our computers so that the slideshow has something to display:

1. From the **Sprites** pane, select the stage thumbnail and then click on the **Backdrops** tab to show the current white project backdrop. Click on the **upload backdrop from file** icon. The following screenshot shows the available **New backdrop** options. The option **upload backdrop from file** is the third icon from the left and looks like a folder with an arrow. You'll also notice these same **New backdrop** options under the stage thumbnail in the **Sprites** pane.

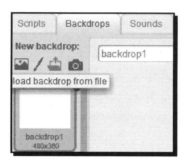

2. Browse your computer's folders until you find your photos and add them to the project. To select multiple files, hold down the *Shift* key while selecting your image files.

 Scratch will autosize the images to fit the stage size of 480 x 360 pixels. If you want to make sure that your image will fit the Scratch stage perfectly, you can use an external graphics editing tool (GIMP, PhotoShop, and others) to crop the image to 480 x 360 pixels prior to importing the image in Scratch.

3. After all the images are imported into Scratch from your computer, you will see a list of backdrop thumbnails in the **Backdrops** pane. To preview each imported image on the stage, click on the thumbnail. This step will confirm that all the images were imported and will be displayed properly.

4. Now, let's work with the names of our images. We're going to display the name of the photo on the stage. On the **Looks** palette, find the **backdrop name** block and click on it to make the name of the image appear on the stage. The following screenshot shows the **Looks** palette and a check mark next to the **backdrop name** block. In my example, this adds the words **bee hive** to the stage.

5. When Scratch imports an image, the backdrop name is derived from the file name of the photo on your computer. In many cases, those file names will be combinations of numbers and dates because that's how your digital camera or phone names them. Fortunately, we can rename the backdrops in Scratch to be something meaningful. As you click on the backdrop thumbnail on the **Backdrops** pane, you will see that the text area in the top-right corner of the image editor contains a name. The following screenshot shows an example of an imported image. Note that the name of the backdrop is **2013-07-08 09.30.3**.

6. Go through your list of imported backdrops and give them meaningful, human-friendly names.

As the following screenshot shows, my project has several photos added, and the default white stage remains as the first backdrop. Like a sprite and its costumes, the stage's backdrops can be edited via the built-in paint editor. The following screenshots show a backdrop on the stage and in the image editor. Should you choose to, you could use one of the image editing tools to manipulate the image in some way. We're not going to modify our imported images, but the option is there should you need to use it.

The list of backdrops is arranged in the order in which they were added, but backdrops can be sorted by dragging and dropping the thumbnail around the **Backdrops** tab. You may want to manually sort your photos because our slideshow will sequentially move through the backdrops and the order in which you display them could become part of the story you tell with your photos.

What just happened?

By importing photos from our individual computers, we create an extremely personal and unique project. Scratch also provides a list of backdrops via the **Choose backdrop from library** icon, which is the first icon under the **New Backdrop** heading.

The **backdrop name** block is a **reporter** block in Scratch and is designed to be used as the value for other blocks. We'll use the **backdrop name** block in a script later in this chapter. The previous exercise gives us a quick and easy caption on the stage as long as we give our backdrops meaningful names. The reporter block can be repositioned on the stage by dragging it around.

An alternative way to accomplish captions and titles is to edit each backdrop to create the captions with the text tool. We've chosen the easier route in our project because we're going to use sound to provide a more detailed explanation of the images, so a description of a word or two will be sufficient.

Adding text directly to the image may appear more polished, but it can be more difficult to maintain. The changing color of the images, for example, may mean you need to reposition the text differently per image or choose a different color for the text. And as we've seen in *Chapter 3, Creating an Animated Birthday Card*, working with the text tool in our images may pose problems to actually changing the text after you save your text.

On the surface, these are not large obstacles and can be overcome. Working in vector mode, for example, will let us edit the text at any time. Therefore, even though we're relying on the backdrop's name and the **backdrop name** block to create a simple caption, it doesn't prevent you from doing something more elaborate.

Let's briefly talk about working with images in Scratch.

Working with images

Working with digital images is a topic worthy of its own book, but Scratch has some built-in image editing capabilities that we can use, and we've seen some of those limited capabilities as we created sprites throughout *Chapter 3, Creating an Animated Birthday Card*. Basically, we can change colors, draw rectangles and circles, insert lines, type text, duplicate areas, and resize, reshape, rotate, and flip images. I'll editorialize for a moment and just say that I think that's an awesome feature set for Scratch to include by default. However, if we want more advanced editing capabilities, we need a more advanced editor. Examples of third-party graphics editors include the following:

- **GIMP**: This is an open source, cross-platform editor available at
  `http://www.gimp.org`
- **Adobe Photoshop**: This is a sophisticated editor offered by Adobe at
  `http://www.adobe.com/products/photoshop.html`
- **MS Paint**: This comes installed with Microsoft Windows
- **Pixelmator**: This is a full-featured app for Macs available at
  `http://www.pixelmator.com`

Scratch imports the popular image formats: PNG, BMP, JPG, GIF, and SVG. If you import an **animated GIF**, Scratch will import each frame as a backdrop or as a costume if you're importing the animation as a sprite. Animated GIF creates animations by combining and cycling through many individual images.

When importing an SVG (vector) graphic, Scratch imports the file as a vector graphic, which means its resolution can be maintained. We introduced vector graphics in *Chapter 3, Creating an Animated Birthday Card*.

Resizing images

The stage in Scratch measures 480 pixels wide by 360 pixels high. In graphic design, we list width first, so an 800 x 600 image is 800 pixels wide. As we learned in *Chapter 3, Creating an Animated Birthday Card*, if we were to look at an image under extreme magnification, we would eventually see individual dots. These dots are pixels and contain all the information the computer needs to display the image on the screen.

Counting pixels becomes important so we can select images that will meet our needs. If we want an image to take up the entire backdrop, we need an image that is at least 480 x 360 pixels to ensure we have an image of acceptable quality.

The problem with using an image that is less than 480 x 360 pixels is that we need to stretch or *upsize* the image in order for it to fill the screen. As we resize an image to a larger size, the pixels are made bigger, and we will begin to see the individual pixels. This effect creates a grainy and unclear image, which is often referred to as a pixelated image.

We don't have to worry about image pixelation when we resize the image to a smaller size from a larger size. Whenever possible, start with a larger image and downsize if needed.

I'll state the exception even at the expense of being obvious. We're working with backdrops in this case, but we can import images as sprites, too. In either case, we may want the imported file to be smaller than the stage, and in those cases, you wouldn't necessarily want to start with a large image.

Using caution while resizing images

The good news is that if we start with an image that is larger than 480 x 360, then we don't need to resize the image at all. Scratch will resize the image to fit within the correct dimensions automatically. Be aware that anytime you allow a computer program such as Scratch to resize your images, you run a great risk of being dissatisfied with the results.

Here's an example. One of the backdrops I started with in the previous exercise was 3504 x 2336 pixels. When I initially uploaded the image via Scratch's paint editor, the imported image was not tall enough, as seen in the following screenshot:

Notice the white space below the image? If you look at the backdrop's thumbnail (highlighted in the screenshot), you will see that the image dimensions are the expected 480 x 360. However, my initial image did not have white space at the bottom.

Here's what's happening. When Scratch receives a big image, it resizes the width to 480 pixels and scales the height appropriately. If the resized height is less than or equal to 360 pixels, no further processing happens; however, the image editor will create an image that is 360 pixels high by filling in the difference with white space. If the resized height is too much, Scratch will crop the bottom of the image to make it fit.

The technical concept at play here is called **aspect ratio**. We'll cite Wikipedia's definition of aspect ratio as "the proportional relationship between its width and its height." The 480 x 360 stage size has a 4:3 aspect ratio. We won't go too far down the aspect ratio path, but if you were to scale an image that is 480 x 360 pixels by setting the width to 4 pixels, the height would proportionally scale to 3. Other common aspect ratios are 3:2 and 16:9, but when Scratch doesn't scale your images as you'd like, the aspect ratio of the image may be the reason.

The bottom line is that if you want to have absolute control over what your image looks like when you import it into Scratch, then use a full-featured image editing software package to crop the image to the correct size before you import it into Scratch.

Have a go hero – importing an animated GIF or vector graphic

In the *Working with images* section of this chapter, I have mentioned that animated GIF and SVG files can be imported into Scratch. These file formats have interesting properties, as we've discussed. Now it's time to see these properties yourself.

The code files in this book include two publically available images that you can use for this exercise. One is `animated gif example.gif` and the other is `yellow bird.svg`.

Import each of these files as both a backdrop and a costume. I recommend that you open a new project as this exercise is a bit tangential to our slideshow project but will prove informative. Make some observations about how Scratch is resizing this image based on how you're trying to use the image in Scratch. The original file size of both sample images is much smaller than the Scratch stage.

The example animation in the book is courtesy of the *Animated Gifs: Fleischer's Bubbles (1922)* series by *The Public Domain Review* website at `http://publicdomainreview.org/2013/09/24/animated-gifs-fleischers-bubbles-1922`.

The example `yellow bird.svg` file was obtained courtesy of the *openclipart* website at `http://www.openclipart.org/detail/190937/yellow-googley-eye-bird-by-ruthirsty-190937`.

Adding slideshow controls to display images

Let's get back to our slideshow. Now that we have our photos imported into Scratch, we need to add a way to click forward and backward through the photos. We'll accomplish this by using one of the arrow sprites included in Scratch's sprite library.

Time for action – flipping through the photos

The Scratch sprite library contains a couple of sample arrows that we can use. However, you may decide to paint your own arrows or import other images. Just keep in mind that we need a left and right arrow.

1. Let's add the **arrow2** sprite from the **Things** folder in Scratch's sprite library. You can find the sprite by clicking on the **Choose sprite from library** in the **Sprites** pane. This sprite points to the right by default, but there's a costume that points to the left, which we'll use in the next step.

2. Let's get an arrow that points to the left into the project. Repeat step 1 and add a second copy of **arrow2**. Click on the **Costumes** tab and select the costume that points to the left. This will give us left and right arrows on the Scratch stage.

If the default color of the arrows blends in with your images, you may want to use the image editor and use the color a shape tool to change the color of the arrow.

3. Position the arrows in the bottom-right corner of the screen.

4. To help keep the arrows straight, rename the left-facing arrow to **Back** and the right-facing arrow to **Next**. Rename the sprite by clicking on the **i** icon on the sprite to display the sprite info pane, as seen in the following screenshot:

5. Let's build the script for the **Next** arrow first. From the **Events** palette, add the **when this sprite clicked** block.

6. From the **Looks** palette, add the **switch backdrop to ()** block and select **next backdrop** from the drop-down list of values.

7. Now, create the same script for the **Back** arrow, but select **previous backdrop** for the value of the **switch backdrop to ()** block.

What just happened?

The scripts we just created for the arrows use the **switch backdrop to ()** block, which is a new Scratch 2.0 block. This simple block has some big ramifications for working with backdrops.

In our script, we used the **next backdrop** and **previous backdrop** values to sequentially move through the backdrops. All backdrops have a number, so if we're currently viewing backdrop number 3, then clicking on the **Next** arrow will display backdrop number 4. And if we're viewing number 4, clicking back will display backdrop number 3.

The **switch backdrop to ()** block also contains a list of all the backdrops in the project, allowing us to select a specific backdrop.

Related backdrop blocks

We've used a couple of the backdrop blocks in our **script** so far. However, there are several backdrop blocks available to us, as listed in the following table. Some backdrop blocks are only available to the stage.

Block name	Location palette	Description	Example uses
switch backdrop to ()	**Looks**	This changes the backdrop on the stage to the one specified. Available attributes are the next background, the previous backdrop, and the name of each stage backdrop.	Can be used to switch the backdrop in a variety of contexts, including creating levels in a game or setting a starting screen.
switch backdrop to () and wait	**Looks** (stage only)	Selects the specified backdrop. This block works in conjunction with the **when backdrop switches to ()** block by waiting for any scripts that start with the **when backdrop switches to ()** block to finish before continuing. Only available to the stage.	Can be used in the same situations as the **switch backdrop to ()** block.

Block name	Location palette	Description	Example uses
backdrop name	**Looks**	Each backdrop has a name. This block allows you to use the name as a value for other blocks and passes the current backdrop's name into the blocks. It's also a reporter block, which means you can show the current backdrop name on the stage by clicking on the checkbox next to the block.	Used when you need to create a script based on a specific backdrop, such as playing a sound or checking for a game level.
backdrop number	**Looks**	A backdrop also has a number to indicate its relative position within the list of backdrops for the stage. The **backdrop number** block can be used to display the number of the current background on the stage or as the value for other blocks. It is only available to the stage.	Similar to the **backdrop name** block.
next backdrop	**Looks**	Go to the next backdrop in the list.	Can be used to create photo slideshows or animations including stop animations.
when backdrop switches to ()	**Events**	Runs the script when the specified backdrop is displayed. The attributes are a list of all backdrops.	Plays a sound based on the backdrop. Runs a script based on a backdrop.
		Allows a sprite to run a script based on switching to the specified backdrop.	

Playing and recording sounds

Scratch provides both a library of sounds that we can incorporate into our project and a way to record our own sounds. We'll start off with a quick exercise to play a sound when we click on the **Next** arrow. Then, we'll explore Scratch's built-in **sound recorder** to narrate our images.

Time for action – adding a sound from Scratch's library

At the moment, we have a script that shows the next background when the user clicks on the **Next** arrow. Let's create a sound effect to signal the next slide:

1. Select the **Next** sprite and add a **play sound ()** block from the **Sound** palette to the script that starts with **when this sprite clicked**.

2. You'll notice that the **play sound ()** block uses a default pop sound. If you click on the **Next** arrow, you'll hear the sound play as the next image loads.

3. Let's choose a new sound from Scratch's library. Click on the **Sounds** tab in the project editor to display a list of sounds associated with the sprite. Then, click on the **Choose sound from library** icon. Look at the following screenshot for reference:

4. The **Sound Library** window will open and display a list of sound categories on the left-hand side. Select **Effects** and then select the **ripples** sound. Click on **OK** to add it to the **Sounds** tab.

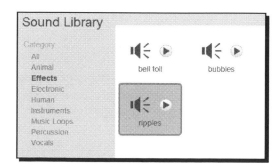

5. Click on the **Scripts** tab.

6. Select **ripples** from the **play sound (pop)** block.

7. Test the script by clicking on the **Next** arrow. Your revised script should look as shown in the following script screenshot:

What just happened?

When our user clicks on the **Next** arrow to change the image, the ripples will signal the image change. Note that when you click on the **Back** arrow, there is no sound. Of course, we can add other sounds to the script, but the critical step is to add them to the sound tab first. Just as sprites and backgrounds, Scratch includes a library of sounds that are freely available for use in our projects.

The sounds are assigned to the sprites. So, if you look under the **play sound ()** block for the **Back** arrow, for example, you'll notice the **ripples** sound is not available.

Next, we'll use the more advanced sound features in Scratch and record our own sound for use in the project.

Time for action – recording sounds in the sound editor

We're going to complete our slideshow by recording some audio to describe each backdrop. This gives our users a richer experience and might be comparable to what you'd experience if you were ever to take a self-guided walking tour.

For the purposes of this exercise, think about a two- or three-sentence description for one of your images. Our basic task will be to add a sprite that will play the correct audio when we click on it. Let's walk through the steps:

1. Sounds are associated with a sprite or the stage, so let's add a sprite that can be used to play the audio we will record. Import **Microphone** from the **Things** category in the **Sprite Library**.

2. Now select the microphone sprite so that we can record our audio. To record new audio, click on the microphone icon in the **Sounds** tab. A new sound called **recording1** is added and selected.

3. Click on the circle icon in the sound recorder to start recording. It is the icon to the left of the **Edit** menu and is shown in the following screenshot:

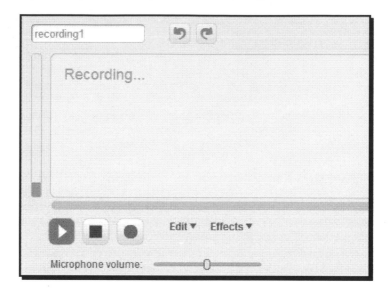

4. When you are finished, click on the square button to stop recording. In the previous screenshot, that's the icon to the left of the record (circle) button.

5. To hear the sound, click on the play button.

6. In order to make our scripting easier and relevant to this project, rename **recording1** to be the name of the image. For example, I made a recording for an image named **Inside bee tree**, so that will be the name for my recording.

7. Now let's write a script that plays our recording when the microphone is clicked. With the microphone sprite selected, click on the **Scripts** tab.

8. From the **Events** palette, add a **when this sprite clicked** block. Then, attach a **broadcast** block.

9. From the **Looks** palette, drag the **backdrop name** reporter block into the value of the **broadcast** block.

10. Now we need to act on the broadcast. Still working with the microphone sprite, add the **when I receive** block to the **Scripts** area. Create a new message that corresponds to the name of the backdrop name. In my example, that name is **Inside bee tree**. Your names will likely be different, but recognize the relationship we're creating here. The name of the backdrop matches the name of the recording.

11. Finish the script by adding the **play sound** block from the **Sounds** palette. Select the recording you just made from the drop-down list of values.

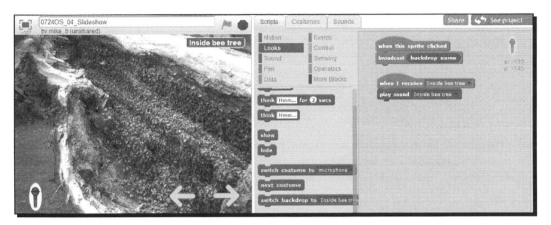

Give it a try. Click through each image in the slideshow and try clicking on the microphone. If you've succeeded, the recording should only play for one image because that's all we've programmed so far.

If you're encountering problems, double check the spelling of the image name, recording name, and broadcast name. Typos will cause this script to fail.

Want to add a second recording? All you need to is to make a new recording, duplicate the **when I receive** script block, and then change the broadcast and sound values accordingly.

What just happened?

We have a lot to cover here, but let's start with the basics. By using Scratch's built-in sound recorder, we were able to narrate an image name. The key to this script is the use of the **backdrop name** reporter block as a value in the **broadcast** block.

Earlier in the chapter, we introduced the **backdrop name** block as a reporter block that always knew the name of the current backdrop. By adding the **backdrop name** reporter block as the value of the **broadcast ()** block, we have created an easier way to broadcast Inside bee tree based on my example in the exercise. This two-block script will work regardless of the backdrop that is currently displayed.

We do have to create a separate **when I receive ()** script for each backdrop we want to narrate. The new broadcast message should match the name of the backdrop you want to play a sound for. Of course, you'll need to record the additional recordings for use in the script.

By using thoughtful naming conventions instead of computer generated defaults, we have a way to keep the backdrop name, recording name, and broadcast name in sync. This will reduce confusion when it's time to manage and troubleshoot our scripts.

Let's take a moment to reflect on a possible variation. Consider the scripts shown in the following screenshot:

The two stacks of blocks on the left are the scripts we built in the previous exercise. The two block script on the right also plays a sound based on the backdrop. We didn't build that one, but it's listed here for discussion purposes.

The critical difference in the scripts shown in the screenshot is *when the sound plays*. Our script enables the user to play the sound on demand. The simpler script will play automatically when the backdrop loads. The user has no say in the decision. However, the script on the right can be used to play an introductory sound when the backdrop loads. We chose to play a generic sound to transition the image, but this discussion introduces an alternative approach.

Understanding sound related blocks

Scratch provides the following blocks for playing sounds:

Block	Palette location	Description	Uses
play sound	**Sounds**	Plays the specified sound. The available attributes are the sounds associated with the sprite or background.	Sound is a generic term that may mean a sound effect, a recording sound, or an imported music file.
play sound until done	**Sounds**	Similar to the **play sound** block, except the script doesn't continue until the sound is finished.	Similar to the play sound block.
stop all sounds	**Sounds**	Stops any sound that is currently playing.	Stops playing sound when a level or background changes.

Editing sounds

The sound editor includes several advanced but easy-to-use options for working with sounds, including copy, paste, and delete.

Time for action – editing a recorded sound

We're going to delete a section of the sound we recorded in the previous exercise. For example, if you recorded a bunch of dead air at the beginning or end, you can use the following exercise to delete it:

1. In the **Sounds** tab, click on your recorded sound to open the sound in the editor.

2. In the sound editor, highlight the area in the sound recorder that you want to delete by clicking and holding the mouse and then dragging the mouse to select the sound you want to remove.

3. Before you delete the selection you can listen to it by clicking on the play button in the editor.

4. From the **Edit** menu, select **Delete**. The following screenshot illustrates the process of deleting a section of a sound:

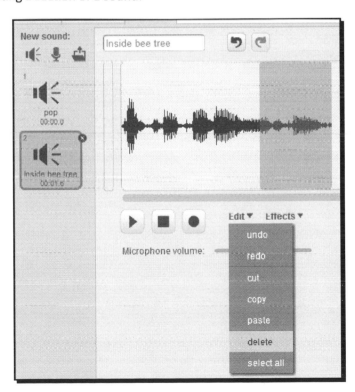

What just happened?

Deleting a section of your recording may be useful, say to trim dead space at the beginning or end of a recording. You can also delete those pesky *ums* and *uhs*.

As you can see in the **Edit** menu, there are several other basic editing options available to us: **cut**, **copy**, **paste**, **delete**, and **select all**.

Time for action – appending a sound

After you listen to a recording, you may realize that you have more to say about it. Let's continue working with our recorded sound:

1. Click on the recording at the point where you want to insert a new sound. The vertical line in the following screenshot shows where the new sound will be added. Note that the screenshot shows that it's possible to add a new recording in the middle of an existing sound.

2. Then, click on the record button and speak.

3. When you're finished, click on the stop button. The newly recorded section will be highlighted when you click on the stop button, as seen in the following screenshot:

4. To preview the new recording, click on the play button. You can keep deleting and recording until you're satisfied with the results.

What just happened?

I find that the hardest thing about recording is actually getting all the words out in a way that makes sense. We've seen how easy it is to record, delete, and edit a sound. As the examples demonstrate, we can edit at the beginning or end or at any point in between.

In our slideshow project, we've been narrating a description of each slide, but we could just as easily record our own sound effects or music.

Time for action – adding sound effects to recordings

After we record our sound, and it's just the way we want it, we can use the sound editor to add effects.

1. Highlight the section of the recording to which you want to apply an effect.

2. Then select an effect from the **Effects** menu to apply it. For example, we could select the **fade in** effect to make the sound start out quietly and gradually get louder.

3. You can expand or reduce the selection by clicking and dragging the edge of the selected sound.

The following screenshot shows the list of effects:

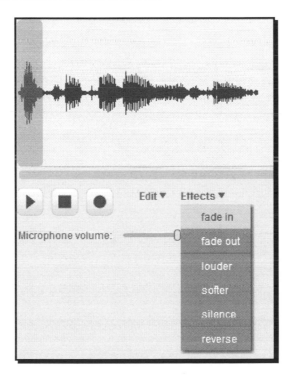

What just happened?

The sound editor includes a list of effects that can be applied to any sound, such as **fade in**, **fade out**, **louder**, **softer**, **silence**, and **reverse**.

Reviewing available sound effects

The following table provides an example usage for each effect:

Effect	Use
fade in	This effect starts the audio quietly and gradually increases the volume.
fade out	This effect starts the audio at a normal volume and gradually decreases the volume until it's quiet.
louder	This effect increases the volume.
softer	This effect decreases the volume of the selection.
silence	This effect silences the audio selection.
reverse	This effect takes the selection and reverses the order with which it is played, which is a good way to create gibberish.

Have a go hero – narrating additional images

Take a moment to record a narration for at least one of the other images in your slideshow and update your scripts to play the narration at the appropriate time. You can also experiment by adding additional sounds based on the backdrop.

Using x and y coordinates to find the position of the mouse's pointer

At this point, our slideshow is full of engaging images and has a rich user experience. We could stop here, but we're going to add one more wrinkle to our show by making the arrows hide and show based on the position of the mouse cursor. We'll build these scripts block by block, so even if the x and y coordinate system is a new concept for you, you'll still have a ready-made example to explore the concept some more.

Time for action – using mouse location to hide arrows

This exercise will add a little bit of glitz to our project, but there's also a functional reason behind our wanting to build this interface. The arrows obstruct a part of our backdrop. Hiding the arrows shows more of the backdrop.

1. To determine when we show or hide the arrows, we need to continually check the position of the mouse. Let's start building the script to do this on the **Next** arrow sprite. Start the script with the **when flag clicked** block. Attach a **forever** block.

2. Inside the **forever** block, add the **if () then, else** block from the **Control** palette.

3. The **if () then, else** block checks to see if a condition is true. To determine when to show the arrows, we're going to check the *x* and *y* position of the mouse. We'll start by adding the **() and ()** block from the **Operators** palette to the value of **if () then, else** to accommodate a check for both *x* and *y* positions.

4. In the left value of the **() and ()** block, add the is greater than (>) block, and then add the is less than (<) block to the value on the right hand side of the **() and ()** block.

5. From the **Sensing** palette, drag the **mouse x** block to the is greater than (>) block and the **mouse y** block the is less than (<) block. The following screenshot shows our script so far:

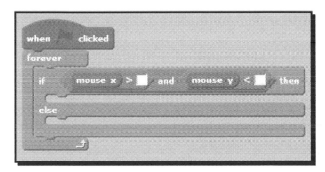

6. Next, we need to replace the empty values of the is greater than (>) and is less than (<) blocks. To do that, we need to determine the *x* and *y* coordinates that will appropriately show the sprites. Consider the following screenshot that shows my **Next** and **Back** arrows with a rectangle around them. If the mouse moves into the rectangle area (the hot zone), as shown in the following screenshot, we will want to display the arrows:

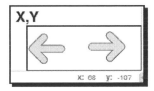

7. As you move your mouse cursor to the right, the *x* value gets bigger. As you move the mouse towards the bottom of the stage, the *y* value gets smaller. The *x* and *y* coordinates of the mouse can be seen in the following screenshot. These values represent the mouse location, which is approximately where the *x* and *y* annotation occurs in the previous screenshot. I'm going to round my values off a bit, and enter 70 in the **mouse x > ()** block script and -105 in the **mouse y < ()** block script. The following screenshot shows the evaluation:

8. Let's finish our script by adding the **show** block to the **if** part of our block and the **hide** block to the **else** part. Our entire script is shown in the following screenshot:

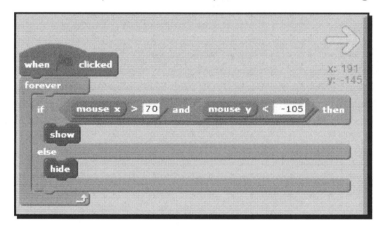

9. Give the script a try by clicking on the green flag and moving your mouse cursor around the screen. If the script behaves as you expect, you can duplicate it and move it to the **Back** arrow sprite.

What just happened?

We created a script to show the **Next** and **Back** arrows depending on the mouse location. We often see this effect on the web, such as while playing or pausing YouTube videos where the video controls are hidden until you mouse over the bottom of the video. The controls are visible when you position your mouse cursor along the bottom of the video. You may wonder how other users will know they need to move their mouse into the corner to display the arrow. We'll address that problem in our next exercise. By using the **() and ()** block, our script was able to check both the *x* and *y* positions of the mouse cursor. Only when both conditions were true did we show the arrows. While we purposely chose to use the coordinates, our values were somewhat subjective in that we can make a larger or smaller hot zone on the stage by altering the coordinates.

If *x* and *y* coordinates are a new math concept for you, you just need to know that each location on the Scratch stage is represented by two numbers. The *x* coordinate identifies the horizontal (left/right) position on the stage while the *y* coordinate identifies the vertical (up/down) position on the stage.

If you're following my example closely, you'll realize that if you move your mouse below and to the right of the stage, the arrows are still visible. That's because the script we created only defined the top and left edges of the hot zone, leaving it an open-ended hot zone.

The stage, however, does have definite boundaries and coordinates. If you move the mouse cursor beyond the boundary of the stage to the bottom-right corner of the project editor, the reported values never show higher than 240 (value of *x*) and -180 (value of *y*). When a user views the project page, this might happen if the user lets the mouse wander below the stage.

Have a go hero – redefining the hot zone

As we've discussed, if the user moves the mouse outside our hot zone, the arrows hide as long as the mouse cursor stays above and to the left of the **Next** and **Back** arrows. If the user moves the mouse below the arrows or to the right of the arrows and outside the stage, then the arrows will still be displayed.

Can you constrain the arrows' hot zone to ensure the arrows are only displayed if the mouse is within the boundary of the stage? You can, and to do this, you'll need to update the arrow scripts to evaluate a second set of *x* and *y* values by modifying this block. **if ((mouse x) > (70) and (mouse y) < (-105))**.

Hints

Add more **() and ()** blocks to the value in the **if () then else** block to check whether the mouse is within the stage boundary. The following expressions check whether the mouse is within the stage boundary:

mouse *x* position < 240

mouse *y* position is > -180

The project files included with the book include a working example of this solution for the **Next** sprite.

Time for action – providing user instructions

Based on our current scripts, it's possible for our slideshow to start with no **Back** or **Next** arrows on the screen because their display is determined by the location of the mouse cursor. That could be confusing to a user. Let's revise our script to provide some user instruction at the start of the project. Select one of the arrows and add a **show** block to the **when flag clicked** block.

1. From the **Looks** palette, add a **say for () secs** block after the **show** block.

2. For the text value of the **say** block, type an instruction to the user (for example, `To advance the slideshow hover over this area.`).

3. Increase the time value in the **say for (2) secs** to 5.

4. Now select the other arrow sprite and add a **show** block after the **when flag clicked** block.

5. This time, add a **wait (2) secs** block after the **show** block. Change the value to 5.

6. Give the script a go by clicking on the green flag.

The following screenshots shows our revised arrow script:

What just happened?

We updated the script for each arrow so that the next and back controls are always visible for at least five seconds when a user starts the project. Both the arrow sprites used the **show** block to always display the arrows. Then we created some user instructions using the **say ()** **for () secs** block.

After the **say () for () secs** block, we go straight to the part of the script that shows/hides the arrows based on where the mouse cursor is positioned. We want the instruction to be displayed for a reasonable amount of time so that our user can read it. The **say () for () secs** block gave us a way to control the timing of our script. Because the block has a seconds value, the message will stay on the screen for the specified time. No other blocks in the script will run as long as the message is displayed on the screen. We solved two problems with one block—user instruction and timing.

When we updated the other arrow sprite, we used the **wait () secs** block in place of the **say () for () secs** block. That's because we don't need both arrows to give instructions, but we do want both arrows to stay on the screen for five seconds.

Displaying a project in presentation mode

Up to this point, we've been viewing our projects in the project editor with the block palette and script areas visible. When our users view the slideshow, they still have a small viewing area, as seen in the following screenshot:

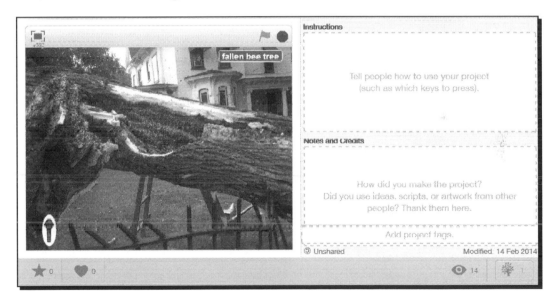

However, Scratch has a way for us to view projects in fullscreen mode.

Time for action – presenting a fullscreen slideshow

Let's check out Scratch's fullscreen presentation mode:

1. The button to enter presentation mode is located in the top-left corner of the project editor. It's the blue square to the left of the project name and below the menus and is shown in the following screenshot:

2. Check out your slideshow by clicking on the blue square.

3. When you've finished viewing the project in fullscreen mode, press the *Esc* key on your keyboard to return to the Scratch interface. You can also click on the blue square to exit fullscreen mode.

What just happened?

Presentation mode allows us to run our projects using a larger viewing area with less screen clutter. And some projects, such as the slideshow we're creating, would look really good displayed in fullscreen mode on our television or large monitor.

Have a go hero – personalizing the slideshow with graphic effects

Right now, we have a functioning slideshow complete with narration. Before you set the family down for a private screening, consider enhancing the transitions between slides with some graphical effects. We covered graphical effects in *Chapter 3, Creating an Animated Birthday Card*.

Pop quiz – reviewing the chapter's concepts

Q1. How big is Scratch's stage?

1. 360 x 480.
2. 480 x 360.
3. 420 x 320.

Q2. After a sound is added to the project, it is available to all sprites via blocks, such as **play sound ()**.

1. True.
2. False.

Q3. What block gives us the name of the current backdrop?

1. **next backdrop**.
2. **backdrop name**.
3. **previous backdrop**.
4. **backdrop #**.

Q4. How would you know where the mouse is located on the screen?

1. The mouse has an *x* coordinate accessible via the mouse *y* block.
2. The mouse has an *y* coordinate accessible via the mouse *x* block.
3. The mouse has *x* and *y* coordinates accessible via the mouse *x* and mouse *y* blocks.
4. You can see the mouse pointer on the screen.

Q5. Which of the following image formats does Scratch support?

1. PNG.
2. GIF.
3. JPG.
4. All of the above.

Summary

How great is Scratch! Not only does it give us an engaging programming environment, it also gives us a whole suite of tools to personalize our projects. In this chapter, the slideshow we created used our personal images. With the click of a button, we brought the images to life with our own recorded voices and with sounds from Scratch's included sound library. And with a little creative programming using the **broadcast** block, we were able to synchronize the backdrops with a specific sound. We ended the chapter with the slightly more advanced concept of using the *x* and *y* coordinate system to locate the mouse and used this as a way to show or hide navigation controls.

Our project used personal photos. However, what we really created was a project that can be remixed into a presentation on any topic: science, favorite Scratch authors, birds found in the backyard, and the list goes on.

In the next chapter, we're going to remix the classic *Pong* game with the game of *Breakout* so we can smash some bricks. We'll introduce variables, conditional statements, and cloning. Cloning is a new Scratch 2.0 feature that allows us to duplicate a sprite and all its associated scripts, costumes, and properties.

6

Making an Arcade Game – Breakout (Part I)

If you spend any time with Scratch, you will encounter a Pong project. In this chapter, we're going to remix that classic arcade game to create our own version of the game Breakout. In Breakout, the player breaks through multiple layers of bricks by hitting a bouncing ball. In this chapter, we'll lay the foundation of the game while in the next chapter we'll make the game more challenging.

In this chapter, we will:

- ◆ Upload a Pong starter project that we will customize
- ◆ Use cloning to create exact duplicates of the sprites that can be individually controlled
- ◆ Find and calculate the sprite direction to program the ball's direction
- ◆ Create and use custom variables to keep score

To help you understand the idea of the game, let's get a brief introduction to Breakout.

Learning about the Breakout game

Breakout is a 1976 **Atari** game that expanded the arcade game **Pong**. In the gameplay, the player hits a ball with a paddle in order to break the rows of bricks. There are eight layers of bricks; every two rows use a different color. From top to bottom, the colors are red, orange, green, and yellow. The player bounces the ball off the paddle or the wall to break the bricks and score points.

Breaking bricks earns points, and the player will have three chances to break all the bricks. The ball speed will increase at defined intervals.

You can read about the history of Breakout on its Wikipedia page. We'll mimic the evolution of Pong into our own variation of a Breakout-style game. By the time we finish this chapter and the next one, we'll have a clear understanding of just how powerful remixing can be.

Let's get started so that we can create our own version of this game.

Discovering Pong

The 1.4 Version of Scratch included a Pong starter project. Now that Scratch 2.0 has moved online, finding those starter projects is more challenging. Therefore, I've included the game in the code bundle of the book. If you haven't already done so, download the book's accompanying code.

Time for action – importing and playing the Pong starter project

Any time we open another person's Scratch project with the intention of remixing it, we need to spend some time understanding the project. This exercise will walk us through the process of uploading a legacy game from our computer and help us discover some of the details. Our first step will be to import, play, and learn about how the existing Pong game works. Let's follow these steps to import and play the game:

1. The starter project has the file name `Pong.sb`. To import it into Scratch, create a new project from the Scratch project editor. Then click on the **File** menu and select **upload** from your computer. Browse and select the `Pong.sb` starter project to create a new project using the uploaded project.

2. Play the game by clicking on the green flag. Move the mouse left or right to control the paddle and hit the ball. Move the mouse up and down the stage, and note that the paddle doesn't move.

3. When you've had enough, stop the game.

4. Let's get some more information about what the ball is doing. With the ball sprite selected, enable the **direction** reporter block by clicking on the checkbox next to the block's name in the **Motion** palette. The value of the direction variable displays on the stage.

5. Play the game again, and note how the value of the ball's direction changes as the ball travels across the stage. When you're done, let the ball hit the red stripe to end the game.

6. Next, we'll examine the paddle's script by clicking on the **paddle** sprite.

7. Enable the **x position** block from the **Sensing** palette by clicking on the checkbox next to the block's name. The **x position** block is also a block and you should now have two stage monitors displayed (one for the ball's direction and one for the paddle's *x* position).

8. Play another game. Watch as the monitor blocks report the direction of the ball and the location of the paddle in real time.

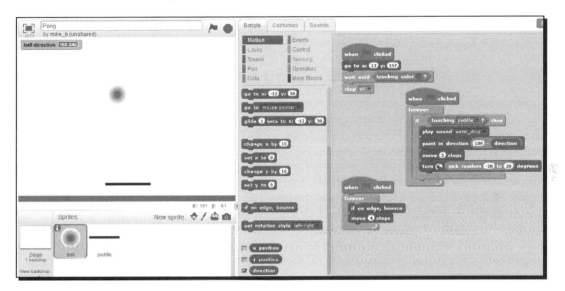

What just happened?

The mission is simple   keep the ball from landing on the red stripe to keep the game alive. The paddle moves based on the movement of the mouse. When you hit the ball, it ricochets off the top and sides of the stage. As we move the mouse to the left, so does the paddle; however, the paddle doesn't respond to up and down mouse movements because the scripts in the game do not specify any action based on the vertical position of the mouse.

We tracked the ball's direction and the paddle's *x* coordinate by enabling the **direction** and **x position** reporter blocks, respectively. These two values highlight the primary variables in Pong. These blocks represent the built-in variables (reporter blocks) in Scratch.

The direction change of the ball is accomplished with the **point in direction** block that executed when the ball touched the paddle. The script calculated the new direction by subtracting the ball's direction from the constant value of **180**.

As the ball bounced off the paddle, the script put a twist on the direction change by turning the ball a random number of degrees between **-20** and **20**. We'll cover the sprite direction in detail later in this chapter.

Remixing a legacy Scratch project

In the previous exercise, we uploaded a Scratch 1.4 project, which can be identified by the .sb file extension. Scratch 2.0 will read this file just fine and actually save it as a Scratch 2.0 file, which uses the .sb2 file extension. In case you're wondering, the choice to start with the legacy version of Pong is a choice made for a few reasons. It's the version I used in the first edition of this book, and it ensures that readers of the book always have the same starting point available to them.

There are Pong starter projects available at scratch.mit.edu, but finding appropriate files to use in one, two, or more years is not guaranteed. Also, the exercise gives a nice lesson using old Scratch file formats—namely, it's possible.

Moving a sprite with the mouse or arrows

The script for the paddle moves the sprite left or right based on the *x* coordinate of the mouse by using the **set x to ()** block. The script reads the *x* coordinate of the mouse via the **mouse x** block and uses that value to set the **x position** of the paddle. The following screenshot shows the script:

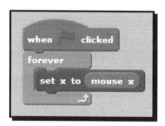

Using reporter blocks to set values

The **mouse x** block enables us to use the current *x* coordinate of the mouse as a value for any block that accepts a numeric value, such as the **set x to ()** block. The **mouse x** block is a reporter block in Scratch. Reporter blocks are the built-in variables that capture the current value of something in Scratch. Other examples include the **direction**, **mouse y**, **loudness**, **x position**, and **y position** blocks. These blocks watch a single value for the sprite they are enabled for. For example, in Pong, the **direction** block always knows what direction the ball is traveling in, and that's the value it reports.

Reporter blocks are the oval-shaped blocks found throughout the palette of blocks in Scratch. And as we'll find out later in this chapter, when we create our own custom variables, Scratch will create a corresponding reporter block.

Variables, whether built-in or custom, provide a way for us to use the value in the reporter block as a value in any of the other Scratch blocks that has an oval shape for a value, as illustrated in the previous screenshot showing the **set x to (mouse x)** block.

Customizing the gameplay of the Pong project

There are a few initial customizations that we will do to make the game easier to use and to avoid potential conflicts with our Breakout game. You might like using the mouse to control the paddle, and that's fine. We're going to walk through the process of changing the paddle control to the left and right arrow keys.

Time for action – adding the left and right arrow controls

Moving the paddle with the mouse works, but users on a laptop may find their built-in mouse difficult to use. Let's revise the paddle script to use the left and right arrows to control movement by following the given steps:

1. Select the paddle sprite from the sprite list.
2. From the **Control** palette, add the **when key pressed** block to the scripts area.
3. Change the value to **left arrow**.
4. From the **Motion** palette, attach the **move () steps** block to the **when left arrow key pressed** block.
5. Change the value to **-10** (negative 10).
6. Repeat steps 4 and 5, but use the right arrow key to move 10 steps.
7. Play the game, and use the arrow keys to move the paddle. The paddle appears to move slowly across the screen.
8. Let's try to take bigger steps. Change the number of steps to a larger number, such as **50**.
9. Clean up the script by removing the original **when flag clicked** block that used the **mouse x** value to control the movement. From the **Motion** palette, uncheck the **x position** block.

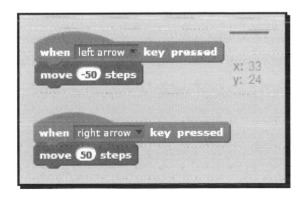

What just happened?

Now we have an alternate way to control the paddle that actually runs the **move () steps** block based on an arrow key event. The **when () key pressed** block continually monitors for a key to be pressed. In our example, we chose to use the left and right arrow keys, but you could have chosen to use any key you wanted.

When the left arrow key is pressed, the paddle moves a value of -50 steps, which moves the sprite to the left. The right arrow key gets a value of 50, which moves the paddle right.

The values in the **move () steps** block, as you might have surmised, match what we expect when we use the coordinate system to locate a sprite. Negative values move left along the *x*-axis; positive values move right.

Evaluating the y position of the ball to end the game

If we look closely at the ball scripts, we see that all scripts will stop when the sprite touches the color red. This signals that the game is over and that the player lost. Red conflicts with one of the primary colors of the bricks we could use later.

Instead, let's evaluate the *y* position of the ball and the paddle to determine if we should end the game.

Time for action – determining if the ball is below the paddle

In the starter project, the game is over when the ball touches the color red, which matches the color of the strip at the bottom of the stage. Red is going to be one of our brick colors, so we'll want to adjust our *game over* condition to be a neutral color.

Basically, we need to determine if the ball falls below the paddle, but in doing so, we're going to encounter some problems that we'll need to solve. Let's follow the given steps:

1. The *game over* condition is set by the ball sprite. So select the ball, and remove the **touching color ()?** block from the value of the **wait until ()** block.

2. Replace **touching color ()?** with the less than block (<) from the **Operators** palette.

3. From the **Motion** palette, find the **y position** block, and add it to the left-hand side of the less than (<) block.

4. From the **Sensing** palette, add the block that reads (**x position**) **of paddle** to the right-hand side of the less than (<) block. Change **x position** to **y position**. The revised script can be seen in the following screenshot:

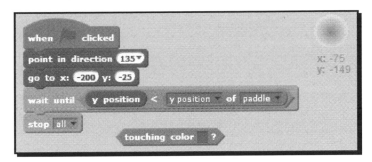

5. Now play the game. Does it behave as you expect? In my game, the game ends when the ball is in the middle part of the stage.

6. To help us debug, turn on the **y position** block for the ball and the paddle so that we can verify that Scratch is correctly following our instructions. See the following screenshot, which is showing a game over condition based on our latest programming changes.

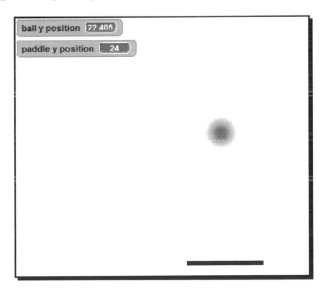

Let's pause and reflect on what we're trying to do compared to what we've done.

What just happened?

We took a working script, made changes, and as a result, no longer have a working game. But our mistakes are not to be punished; they are to be learned from.

We expect the paddle, which is positioned near the bottom of the stage, to have a **y position** of approximately **-175**. In reality, the **y position** of the paddle is closer to **24**. Your position may vary a bit, but it's clearly nowhere close to what we expect.

So, what's wrong with the paddle?

To answer that question, we need to know that Scratch determines the *x* or *y* position of the sprite based on the center of the sprite.

Time for action – adjusting the center of a sprite costume

Let's edit the paddle in the image editor to see where the center of the paddle is by following the given steps:

1. Look closely at the costume in the paint editor. You likely see a vertical scroll bar in the editor, and the paddle is not visible unless you scroll down. In the middle of the screen is a cross mark.

2. The problem is looking straight at us. The center for this costume is not actually on the black paddle. It's above the actual paddle. Let's redefine the center by clicking on the set costume center icon, located at the top-right of the paint editor.

3. When you click the set costume center icon, two intersecting lines appear on the image canvas. The current center is at the intersection of those two lines.

4. To reset the center, click on the intersection of the lines with your mouse, and drag the point down to your paddle, as illustrated in the following screenshot:

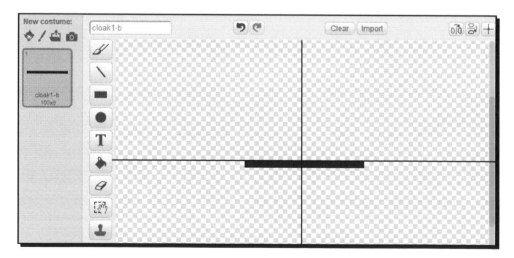

5. To save the change, just click anywhere on the paint editor canvas.

6. On the stage, the paddle will reposition itself to the middle of the stage. Drag the paddle back to the bottom of the stage to put it in its place.

7. Now, play the game again. This time the game over check works as expected.

What just happened?

For some reason, the center of the paddle costume was disconnected from the visible part of the sprite. Because neither you nor I created the original project, we can only speculate why the original game's author made that choice, and speculation is not going to help us. By adjusting the center of the sprite to be on the sprite, our new game over evaluation works as expected. When the *y* position of the ball is less than the *y* position of the paddle, all scripts stop—our current game over condition.

Have a go hero – using the costume center in projects

As Pong demonstrates, the center of the costume determines the location of the sprite in terms of the *x* and *y* coordinates. Sprites also rotate around the costume's center. And in another use, when you tell a sprite to go to the position of another sprite, the first sprite goes to the center of the second sprite.

 In Scratch 2.0, you must set the centers of your costumes manually when you create a sprite or costume.

In theory, setting the center of a costume is a straightforward idea. However, in practice, adjusting the center of your sprite's costume could have dramatic, interesting, or confounding consequences. Here's a quick script courtesy of the Scratch Wiki to clearly demonstrate costume centers:

Draw a square, and fill it with a color. Set the center to the middle of the square. Animate the sprite using the following script. Then adjust the center of the sprite to be on a corner of the sprite. Compare the rotation differences.

Cloning to create identical sprites

We're going to use a Scratch 2.0 feature called **cloning** to easily create rows of bricks that the player breaks during gameplay.

Time for action – drawing bricks

To clone a brick, we need to first make a brick. We'll use the paint editor to do that. We'll use this single brick to build a continuous row of bricks across the width of the stage in a later exercise. Let's follow the given steps to create a brick:

1. Create a new sprite with the paint new sprite icon, and then convert the sprite to the vector mode.

2. Use the rectangle tool to create a solid yellow shape.

3. Draw the rectangle to be 48 pixels wide and 25 pixels tall. To see the current size of the rectangle, look at the thumbnail of the costume to see the current size. The width of 48 pixels will allow us to create 10 blocks to span the width of the stage. We have more flexibility in the actual height.

4. The following screenshot shows the costume thumbnail with the image dimensions:

5. You can resize the height and width of the shape by dragging the borders of the rectangle. This step takes some finesse to get the right size.

6. Don't forget to set the costume center.

What just happened?

This step actually takes some planning as the exercise suggests. We want the row of bricks to span the entire width of the stage, which is 480 pixels. So a 48 pixel wide block will take 10 blocks to span the stage.

We drew the brick using Scratch's built-in image editor, and even though it's a bit awkward, it is possible to resize the sprite to a target size if the image is in vector format. An alternative way to create a block to a specific size would be to use a third-party image editor to create the image and then import that image into Scratch.

Time for action – cloning bricks

Our task is to take the single brick and continuously duplicate it until we create two solid rows of yellow bricks that span the width of the stage. As we work through the exercise, we'll make a couple of calculations to accomplish the task, and we'll tie it all together after we create the script. Let's follow the given steps for cloning bricks:

1. Start the script with a **when flag clicked** block, and add the **show** block.

2. We need to specify the starting point of the blocks, so add the **go to x: y: ()** block from the **Motion** palette. We're going to assume a starting point on the left-hand side of the stage. Set the **x:** value to **-216** and the **y:** value to **25**.

3. Add a **repeat ()** block, and change the value to **10**.

4. From the **Control** palette, add the **create clone of ()** block, and choose **myself** from the drop-down list.

5. Add a **go to x: () y: ()** block to the **create clone of ()** block.

6. From the **Operators** palette, drag the addition block (**+**) block into the **x:** value. From the **Motion** palette, add the **x position** block to the first value of the addition block. Then change the second value of the addition block to **48**. Our calculation reads **x position + 48**, where **48** is the brick size.

7. To the **y:** value, add the **y position** block from the **Motion** palette.

8. Copy the **go to x: () y: ()** block in step 2 and place it after the **repeat ()** block. Change the **y:** value to be the sum of the **y position + 25**. Duplicate the **repeat ()** block, and add it to the bottom of our stack.

9. Add a **hide** block to the end of the stack. The following screenshot shows the script we just built:

What just happened?

We have a lot to sort out in this stack of blocks. Let's start with the positioning of the first brick. We know that the left edge of the stage is represented by an *x* coordinate of -240. When Scratch displays the coordinates of a sprite, it uses the center of the sprite, which means we can divide the length of our sprite in half to get its center point (24 pixels). The calculation to find the starting *x* position becomes *-240 + 24 = -216*.

The starting *y* coordinate is somewhat arbitrary in the current script. Depending on how many rows of bricks you add to the level and how tall you make each brick, you may need to revise the starting height.

Inside the **repeat (10)** block, the **create clone of (myself)** block duplicates the brick ten times. The **go to x: ((x position) +(48)) y: (y position)** block advances across the stage by a value of 48. The number **48** represents the width of the block we created.

With each loop through the **repeat (10)** block, the script creates a new clone that is 48 pixels to the right of the previous clone. We use the *x position + 48* calculation because the **x position** block always knows the current position of the sprite, and we place block two relative to the position of block one, and block three relative to block two, and so on until the stage width is filled.

The script uses another **go to x: () y: ()** block to position the second row of bricks. This time, we change the *y* value by 25, or the height of one brick, but we use the sprite's current **y position + 25** to get the starting height. This way if we do change the starting height of the yellow brick, we only have to change the **y:** value in the first **go to x: () y: ()** block. That's the reason we built the script using the **y position** block in all of the **go to x: () y: ()** blocks even though the height only changes once. It will make future maintenance and improvements a bit easier.

The second **repeat (10)** block builds the second row of bricks across the stage and works in the same way as the first **repeat ()** block we built.

The end result of our programming is two yellow horizontal rows of bricks. Because our bricks rely on the most rudimentary designs, the row appears as a continuous strip of yellow, but rest assured, they are individual bricks. The more effort and design you apply to the brick, the more realistic it can look. We're not going to get bogged down in design. You can handle those revisions later.

Dealing with the cloned sprite

In our script, each **repeat ()** block clones itself 10 times to fill the width of the stage, and at the very end of the stage, we hide the original yellow brick sprite. If we did not hide this sprite, we would have an eleventh brick on the second row. Because the clones inherit all the properties of the original and become separate instances, we no longer have a use of the original sprite we cloned.

You may be asking, "Why don't we repeat the cloning steps nine times and leave the original block showing?"

We could have done that and my early version of the game did that. However, that approach will convolute our future scripts because we'd have to write one script to break the clones and one script to break the sprite.

Time for action – breaking bricks when I start as a clone

Cloning works in Scratch in two major steps. First, we need to duplicate the sprite. Second, we write the scripts that tell the clone what to do.

We created the clones in the previous exercise. Now, let's break the bricks by following the given steps:

1. From the **Control** palette, add the **when I start as a clone** block from the **Events** palette to the scripts area of the yellow brick sprite to handle the cloned sprites.

2. We'll need to continuously check if the ball and the clone touch so that we know when the brick is supposed to break.

3. Start with a **forever** block, and then add the **if () then** block from the **Control** palette.

4. Inside the **if () then** block, add the **delete clone** block from the **Control** palette, which will represent the breaking brick.

5. From the **Sensing** palette, add the **touching ()?** block to the value of the **if () then** block, and select **ball** as the touching value.

The following screenshot shows the new script (on the right-hand side) and the script we built in the previous exercise because the script on the left-hand side creates the clone, while the other script defines what happens to the clone after it is created.

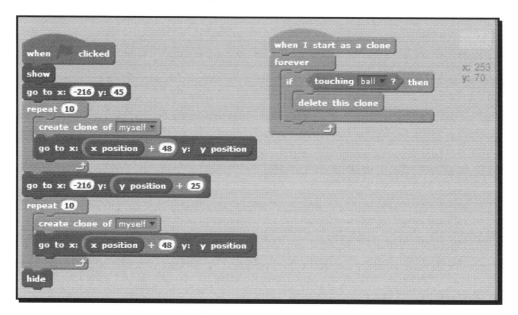

What just happened?

If you haven't already done so, play this game so that you can see what happened. Don't worry about what the ball is doing yet.

The script we created for **when I start as a clone** continually checks each clone to see if it is touching the ball sprite. If the ball and the clone touch, we delete the clone. And in the context of our game, deleting the clone is the same as breaking the brick.

What happens when the ball breaks the bricks, in terms of our game, is going to be the subject of many exercises and also provides endless customizations.

Cloning explained

As our two previous exercises demonstrated, a clone in Scratch 2.0 is a duplicate of the sprite being cloned. A clone inherits the costumes, variables, and scripts of the parent sprite; however, the clone can be modified after it's created. This makes cloning a very powerful resource for Scratch programming.

Here's a simple example that shows a clone being modified after it was created. I used this in my early versions of the cloning bricks exercise to ensure that I was really getting 10 bricks.

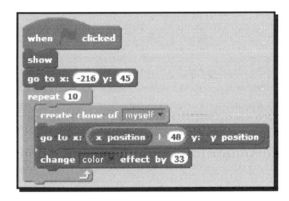

In the previous screenshot, the **change (color) effect by (33)** block changes the color of the sprite, and we end up with a pattern of differently colored bricks.

Rapid fire shooting with cloning

We're using clones to replicate rows of bricks, and each clone can be acted upon independently, but consider the challenge of an Asteroid-like game where you shoot falling objects. Prior to Scratch 2.0, we could only fire one shot at a time. The shot would have to miss or hit the target before reloading.

Cloning allows you to shoot a continuous stream of bullets at the target. We can illustrate the concept using our existing game of Breakout. The following two scripts show how we could make our paddle rapid-fire balls at the bricks.

To make the paddle clone the ball (that is, a bullet), use the script in the following screenshot. The **create clone of ()** block is using a sprite named **ball2** because I duplicated the ball sprite, so I didn't modify the sprite in my game and make inadvertent mistakes.

The following screenshot shows the **when I start as a clone** block that would be attached to the ball. The critical control point of the script is the **repeat until ()** block that will move the clone (the ball in this example) ten steps until it touches the stage edge or a yellow brick.

These two scripts could be duplicated and modified for any shooting game you might create.

Cloning related blocks

The following table shows the available cloning blocks in Scratch:

Block	Description	Example usage
when I start as a clone	This block allows the clone to act independently of the parent sprite. It waits until the clone is created to run.	◆ Detects when a clone collides with sprite ◆ Moves the clone ◆ Changes the clone's appearance

Block	Description	Example usage
create clone of ()	This block clones the sprite running the block or another sprite. It specifies the sprite to be cloned in the drop-down list.	◆ Rapid-fire a never-ending supply of bullets ◆ Create fireworks ◆ Create multiple copies of a sprite
delete this clone	This block gives you a way to programmatically delete the clones.	◆ After the clone and sprite collide ◆ After the game is over

Ricocheting with the point in direction block

In a game of Pong or Breakout, controlling the ball's movement is critical, and as a game designer, you can make the ball move in a predictable way or choose not to. Let's run several exercises that explore the current ball movement and then revise the script.

Time for action – changing a sprite's direction

Why does the **point in direction ()** block use the calculation **180 - direction**? Let's answer that question by experimenting with some new directions as given in the following steps:

1. Select the ball sprite from the sprites list, and find the script that contains the **point in direction ()** block. See the following screenshot:

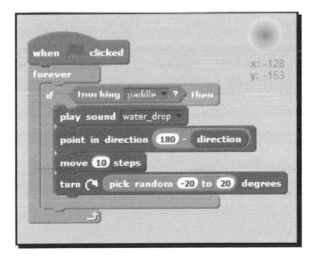

Find the calculation used to redirect the ball and change 180 to 90:

1. Play the game and observe the results.

2. Let's simplify the direction change. Drag the green number block that currently contains the calculation **90 - direction** out of the value of the **point in direction()** block. You can drag it down to a blank spot in the scripts area.

3. Change the value of the **point in direction** block to **180**. Click the green flag to play. Observe the results. The ball should always fall through the paddle and to the bottom of the screen.

4. Change the value of the **point in direction ()** block to **0**. Click the green flag to play. This time the ball bounces back up when it hits the paddle.

5. Drag the **turn clockwise** block to a blank spot in the scripts area so that it doesn't run when we play the game.

6. Click the green flag. Each time the ball hits the paddle, it bounces straight up.

7. Restore the **180 - direction** block to the **point in direction ()** block. The script should look like the following screenshot:

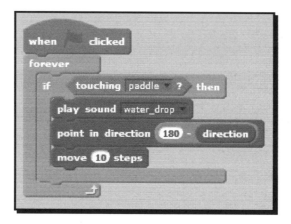

What just happened?

In the original **point in direction ((180) – (direction))** block calculation, the script calculated a new direction by subtracting the ball's current position from 180. For example, if the ball's direction is 121, the calculation subtracts 121 from 180 to get 59. Therefore, the value of the **point in direction ()** block becomes 59, and that's the new direction of the ball. The script also added a random turn.

The original calculation always seems to bounce the ball off the paddle and put it in play. When we changed our calculation to use **90 - direction**, the ball behavior became much more erratic and may have failed to bounce off the paddle.

When we simplified our direction with a value of 180, the ball never appeared to bounce off the paddle. In reality, however, the ball did bounce off the paddle; it just bounced down.

When we set the direction to 0, the ball bounced off the paddle as expected; however, it bounced straight up with a bit of an angle. The **turn () degrees** block ensures the ball doesn't bounce straight up because it's turning a random number of degrees.

You may note that I didn't put the **turn () degrees** block back into the script. I'm choosing to leave it out for now, so that I can have a more predictable bounce as we continue to build scripts. After we get things working, this would be a good effect to add back.

Figuring out the direction

The **point in direction ()** block has several prepopulated values available. Understanding what those values mean to Scratch will help us move the ball in the right direction. The block does not use a 360 degree circle. Instead, the values are 180 to -180, and that can be confusing. As a reference point, -90 as a block value would be equivalent to 270 if we were talking about a 360 degree circle.

The following table outlines how the predefined values move the sprite:

Direction value	Movement
0	Up
90	Right
-90	Left
180	Down

The **point in direction ()** block accepts custom values as well. Use the four default values as a guide to determine which way the sprite will move.

Time for action – setting the starting position and the direction

Let's take what we learned about the **point in direction ()** block and apply it to the starting position of the ball. We'll also set the starting coordinates because the ball currently starts above the row of bricks. Let's follow the given steps for setting the starting position and the direction:

1. Change the starting *x* and *y* coordinates in the **go to x: y:** block to be **-200** and **-25**. The value **-25** will keep us below the bricks, and **-200** positions the sprite on the left-hand side of the stage.

2. We want to make sure the ball moves down at the start of the game. Add a **point in direction ()** block. Change the value to **135**. The revised script can be seen in the following screenshot:

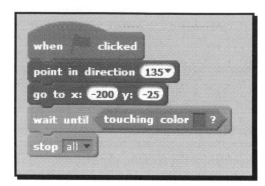

3. As you play the game, note the direction being reported in the direction stage monitor.

What just happened?

The initial starting position of the ball was above the yellow bricks, so our first tweak starts the ball below the bricks on the left-hand side of the stage. By adding the **point in direction ()** block, we can control the starting trajectory with a direction of **135**.

Did you notice the ball's direction? The ball always approaches the paddle at either 135 or -135 and leaves the paddle at 45 or -45. When the ball bounces on the edge of the stage, it leaves in the opposite direction, so it will bounce at -45 or 45.

Without the turn block adding a random rotation to the block, the movement of the ball is predictable, and you eliminate the possibility of getting awkward angles as the ball bounces off the paddle. We can also clearly see our calculations in action.

Time for action – ricocheting off bricks

Right now, the ball bounces off the edge and ricochets off the paddle, but it continues passing through the bricks. We're going to change that behavior by making the ball bounce off the bricks. Let's follow the given steps:

1. Select the yellow brick sprite. Add a **broadcast ()** block to the script that checks if the brick touches the ball, and create a new message called **bounce**. See the following screenshot:

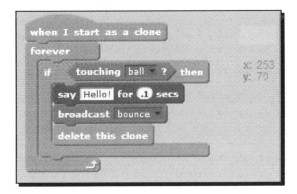

Troubleshoot with the say block

If you're having problems with a script or you want to be sure a certain part of the script is working, you can add a **say ()** block, as seen in the previous screenshot. When the condition is met, a quick **Hello!** appears on the screen.

---

2. Select the ball sprite, and add the **when I receive** block to the scripts area.

3. Attach a **point in direction ()** block.

4. We're going to do a calculation inside the **point in direction ()** block to redirect the ball back to the paddle. Add a multiplication (*) block from the **Operators** palette. Then add a subtraction (-) block to the left-hand side of the multiplication block.

5. Add a **direction** block to the left-hand side of the subtraction block, and enter 180 to the first box. Multiply that by **-1**. See the following screenshot:

What just happened?

This piece of our game creates a realistic response when the ball breaks a brick. Our first step was to send a broadcast message when the brick touches the ball. This coordinates the ball's change in direction.

We then told the ball to act on the broadcast with a new trajectory that we calculated in the **point in direction ((direction) - (180) * (-1))** block. Now, here is where our exercise gets interesting. This calculation is a bit more complicated than changing the direction when the ball bounces off the paddle.

Let's run through a simple calculation. Remember, the ball is traveling at +/- 45 as it leaves the paddle and +/-135 as it approaches the paddle. This means that the ball approaches the bricks at +/-45. So, if the ball is traveling in a direction of 45 and hits a brick, then the new direction is calculated as ((45-180)*-1) or 135. If you run the calculation for a ball direction of -45, the new direction becomes -135.

This creates the same bounce pattern as the ball hitting the paddle; however, we achieve it with a variation of our direction calculation for bouncing off the paddle. The end result is that the ball is reflected away from the bricks and towards the paddle.

Conditional statements

If we go back to the **when I start as a clone** script in use by the brick, we see an **if () then** block that checks to see if the brick is touching the ball, and it's wrapped in a **forever** block. We first reviewed **forever** blocks in *Chapter 2, A Quick Start Guide to Scratch*. While the **forever** block always runs, the code in the **if () then** block only runs when the condition is true. Scratch provides several other conditional blocks for use in our scripts, as seen in the following table:

Block	Description	Example usage
if ()	This block is deprecated in Scratch 2.0 and is replaced by the **if () then** block. You may encounter this block if you're editing a Scratch 1.4 project.	◆ See the **if () then** block
if () then	This block evaluates an argument, and if the argument is true, then the code runs.	◆ Compare values ◆ Control a sprite ◆ Check input
if () then else	This block evaluates an argument, and if true, the code in the **if** block runs. If false, the code in the **else** block runs.	◆ Run code based on the checked value such as checking a player's "lives" in a game ◆ Evaluating the player's score

Block	Description	Example usage
repeat until ()	This block evaluates an argument, and if it's `false`, the code runs.	◆ Position a sprite on the screen ◆ Repeat a script for a specified time or interval
wait until ()	When the specified condition is `true`, run the blocks following the **wait until** block.	◆ Check for game over ◆ Wait for a specific variable value before running a script

The conditional blocks control when and if something happens, so we find them in the **Control** palette.

Conditional statements in real life

Conditional statements are an integrated part of our everyday, non-programming thought process in that we evaluate our environmental inputs and take action based on the results. Here's an example. You want to cross the street. If there are no oncoming cars, you cross the street. If there are oncoming cars, you wait and check again.

If we reframe our example of crossing the street into a programming statement using one of Scratch's conditional statements, we might say:

◆ If there are no cars coming, then cross the street

◆ If there are cars coming, do not cross the street; else, cross the street

◆ You'll wait until there are no cars coming before crossing the street

◆ When you receive a walk signal, cross the street

Defining a variable to keep score

How do we know how good we are if our game doesn't keep score? The next step in our project is to add points each time we break a brick and display the value on the stage.

Before we begin, turn off any remaining monitors from the stage because we no longer need to see them.

Time for action – adding a score variable

To keep score, we need to set up a variable and add a conditional statement to increment the score when the ball touches a brick. Let's follow the given steps to add a score variable:

1. From the **Data** palette, click on the **Make a Variable** button to display the **New Variable** dialog box.

2. Type the word Score, and select the **For all sprites** option.

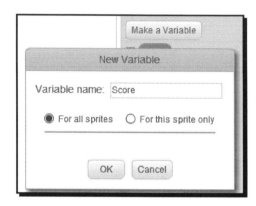

3. Click on **OK** to add the variable. The **Data** palette displays several new blocks, and the **Score reporter** block automatically displays a monitor on the stage.

4. Position the score monitor somewhere on the stage where it won't interfere with the gameplay, such as in a bottom corner.

5. We will increase the score when a brick breaks, so let's work with the yellow brick sprite. Add the **change () by ()** block from the **Data** palette after the **broadcast (bounce)** block in the **when I start as a clone** script. The default block values of **score** and **1** are correct.

6. Click on the green flag and play the game. Each time the ball breaks a brick, the score increments. Play the game several times and note that we have a running score.

7. We need to reset the score to 0 at the beginning of the game. From the **Data** palette, add the **set () to ()** block between the **when green flag clicked** and **show** blocks. The default block values of **score** and **0** are correct.

8. Play the game a few times. The score resets to zero each time you click on the green flag.

9. The following screenshot shows the two revised scripts for the yellow brick sprite:

What just happened?

Each time the ball touches the brick, we Increase the score by 1 and display the value on the stage. At the start of each game, we reset the score to 0, so that the player doesn't add to the score from the previous game.

When we created the score variable, we set it for all sprites because as we build upon this game, we will add different colored bricks, and this will allow all brick sprites to adjust the score. Let's review the two different variable options: **For this sprite only** and **For all sprites**.

Setting variables For all sprites

When we make a variable for a sprite, we can select the **For all sprites** option. This makes a global variable, which means that all our sprites can access the value stored in the variable. This has a couple of implications.

All sprites can change the value of a global variable; therefore, it can be difficult to track problems when they occur because we have to investigate each script in each sprite to find all the places that may be affecting our project. The bigger our project gets, the harder it can be to keep track of global variables.

We may also end up programming in some unintended consequences, such as adding points to our score each time we press the right arrow key. Sure, we can track those mistakes down, but if we can avoid creating those problems, we should.

Working with too many global variables will quickly complicate your scripts because each sprite has access to the variables, and the **Data** palette will fill up with variable options.

Setting variables For this sprite only

In contrast to the global variable, Scratch allows us to create a variable, **For this sprite only**. Programmers often call this a local variable because it can only be accessed by the sprite you assigned it to.

It's a good programming habit to use a local variable whenever you can because it will keep your **Data** palette and variables organized. It also reduces the risk of inadvertently setting your variable's values by an unrelated sprite.

Have a go hero – creating a graphical effect for the bricks

What happens when the ball breaks the brick? Our game currently hides the brick, but that's not too exciting. Take this opportunity to make the brick do something when it's hit by the ball. Here are some suggestions to get you started: change color, show a cracked brick, explode the brick, and so on.

Pop quiz – reviewing the chapter

Q1. When cloning in Scratch, the clone inherits the original sprite's:

1. Costumes.
2. Scripts.
3. Variables.
4. All of the above.

Q2. The center of a costume is always at the center of the visible sprite.

1. True.
2. False.

Q3. What is another way to state Scratch's direction of -90?

1. 270 degrees.
2. 340 degrees.
3. 135 degrees.
4. 45 degrees.

Q4. Why would you want to use a local (**For this sprite only**) variable compared to a variable for all sprites?

1. Local variables are accessible to all sprites.
2. Local variables minimize clutter and future mistakes.
3. There is no reason to use local variables.
4. Local variables are easier to define.

Q5. Which of the following block commands represents a conditional statement?

1. **move (10) steps**.
2. **forever**.
3. **if () then**.
4. **repeat 10**.

Summary

Right now we have a playable version of our Breakout game with a solid foundation. The ball breaks bricks, we keep score, and there's a game over condition. However, there are several very important concepts introduced in this chapter that will make you Scratch programming ninjas, including cloning, conditional statements, and variables. The game, however, is not very challenging yet.

In the next chapter, we'll continue building our Breakout game to create a more challenging gameplay by increasing the ball speed and adding more bricks. We'll learn how to condense our scripts by turning duplicate blocks of code into a reusable custom block. We'll also take a look at cloud variables to keep score, which is another one of Scratch 2.0's featured additions.

7
Programming a Challenging Gameplay – Breakout (Part II)

We ended Chapter 6, Making an Arcade Game – Breakout (Part I) with a framework for the Breakout game. Basically, we're breaking bricks and keeping scores in the framework. The game ends if we miss the ball. In this chapter, we're going to develop the game by adding challenging elements such as increased ball speed and a shrinking paddle. By the time we finish the chapter, we'll have a strong foundation that you can continue developing.

Our objectives include:

- ◆ Making incremental changes to the game, including multiple lives and ball speed
- ◆ Implementing custom blocks as a way to consolidate duplicate scripts
- ◆ Understanding how to use Boolean blocks to control program flow
- ◆ Creating variables that use cloud data
- ◆ Debugging and considering alternative solutions

If you've already made a bunch of changes to your game, which will make it difficult for you to follow this chapter, you can open the project from *Chapter 6, Making an Arcade Game – Breakout (Part I)*, from the book's source files, and continue working through this chapter.

Implementing lives

Up until now we have seen that the Breakout game ends when the ball falls below the paddle, which occurs when the player misses the ball. In the original gameplay, the player has three turns to clear as many bricks as possible across the two levels.

Time for action – adding a variable to track lives

As we make the game more difficult, it will be appropriate to provide the player with more than one opportunity to clear the game. We'll do this by tracking the player's lives, as shown in the following steps:

1. Create a variable named `lives`. You can create it **For all sprites**.

2. Let's set the starting value of the new variable at the start of the game. Select the **ball** sprite. Then, add a **set () to ()** block to the **when flag clicked** stack, which sets the ball's initial position and direction.

3. Select the **lives** variable and enter the value 3.

4. Next, we need to change the logic that ends the game to check for life. To do this, detach the **stop (all)** block from the **wait until (y position) < (y position) of (paddle)** block.

5. Instead of stopping everything, let's decrease the value of the **lives** variable. Add a **change () by ()** block to the bottom of the stack. Select the **lives** variable and enter a value of `-1` in the **by** value.

6. Add a **wait until ()** block from the **Control** palette to the bottom of the **change (lives) by (-1)** block.

7. Using the **() = ()** block from the **Operators** palette, make the **wait until ()** block evaluate if **lives = 0**.

8. Then, add the **stop (all)** block to the end of the stack.

Play this game and miss the ball on purpose. Does your game ever end? How about the lives value—does it ever reach zero? No. We have a bug.

The following screenshot shows our current script:

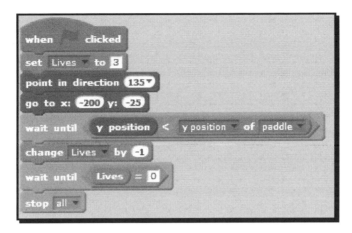

Let's pause a bit to examine this script and identify the bug.

What just happened?

Adding the **lives** variable was straightforward. We defined the variable by assigning it a starting value 3. Each time the player misses the ball, **change (lives) by (-1)** will run and reduce the number of lives available to the player. When there are no more lives left, the game ends. At least, that's how we want our project to work. To understand why it's not working as expected, we have to figure out how a **wait until ()** block works.

By this point, we know that the code after the **wait until ()** block does not run until the value evaluates to true. What's happening in our script is that if we miss the ball once, the **lives** variable is properly reduced. The script also evaluates the **wait until (lives = 0)** block, which amounts to false; therefore, our game continues correctly.

When the player misses the ball the second time, we see our bug. The problem is that the **wait until ()** block will run only once; therefore, the code to reduce the variable by -1 never runs more than once, ensuring that the **lives** variable remains at a value of 2.

We need to rewrite the script to get better control over the **wait until ()** blocks.

Time for action – checking for game over

There's going to be more than one way to address our "game over" bug, and that shouldn't surprise you by now. We're going to approach this problem with the **forever** block.

Let's see what we can do by performing the following steps:

1. First, detach the first **wait until ()** block from the script and add the **forever** block in its place.

2. Add two **if () then** blocks to the **forever** block because we will evaluate two unique values.

3. The first **if () then** block should evaluate the **y position < y position of (paddle)** statement.

4. Add the **change (Lives) by (-1)** block to the first **if () then** block we just added.

5. Make the second **if () then** block evaluate **lives = 0**.

6. Add the **stop (all)** block to the second **if () then** block we just added.

7. Play the game and allow the ball to miss the paddle, and then watch your lives quickly drop to zero. Now, we've found another bug. The following is a screenshot of our current script:

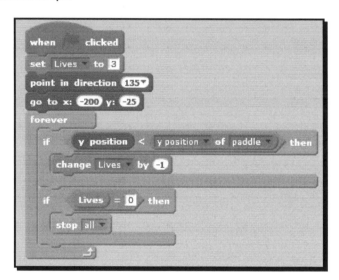

8. This bug can be overcome by adding a copy of the **go to x: () y: ()** block to the **change (lives) by (-1)** block. The following screenshot shows the revision:

What just happened?

Scratch, like any other programming language or computer application, is designed to do exactly what you tell it to instead of what you think it should do. In addition, we don't know how far that gap is until we snap some blocks together and run the code.

We started this exercise knowing that we had to fix our **wait until ()** blocks because they didn't sufficiently control the flow of our script. The fix was to use a combination of a **forever** block and two **if () then** blocks.

The second big problem we encountered was that once the ball fell below the paddle, the ball remained below the paddle and depleted the player's lives. The ball never went back into play. The **go to x: (-200) y: (-25)** block, which we added after we reduced the player's life, put the ball back into play like it was at the beginning of the game. Even though we are going back to the original starting position, you can choose to randomize the new starting position to add some unpredictability.

Evaluating multiple programming solutions

Let's pause for a brief discussion on revising our script. I was provided with an alternative script to fix the bug of reducing the player's life. As the solutions go, the script that was provided to me is concise and is visible in the following screenshot:

It has some benefits in which it doesn't duplicate some blocks and uses one of the original **wait until ()** blocks. The question about whether this is a better solution or not is a subjective debate, as it doesn't inherently work any better than the original revision that we did in the exercise. That's the point of our diversion. When you're faced with constructive criticism, you get to choose how you're going to accept the critique in most cases. Naturally, parents and teachers get to impose their will on the people they teach, but independent readers always have a choice about how these scripts come together.

Sometimes a functional script trumps someone else's beautiful solution. Unless I'm fixing a bug or my original solution was just absolutely hideous, I don't make changes to my script just because someone else has a "better" solution. There are some differences that make me consider revising the script in the previous exercise, and it has to do with the starting location and direction of the ball.

We programmed our ball to start at point (-200,-25) and after the player misses, we send the ball back to the same place. The ball, however, will restart in its previous direction, which may actually be -135. If it's -135, it will bounce off the side of the stage after being put back into play (that is, after the player misses the ball). Now, the question is—does that matter? If it does, then you need to consider revising the script. However, what if we wanted the ball to start at a specific location, but go to a random starting position after the player misses the ball? In that case, the proposed solution in the previous screenshot will make our change a bit harder, though not impossible.

Hopefully, you will see that the decision to revise a script is not always a simple right or a wrong option. Rather, these changes have complications and ramifications. The decision about which solution to implement is yours.

Have a go hero – programming a character's health

Our Breakout game uses lives to track the number of chances a player gets to win the game. When the player misses the ball, the game takes away a chance. A closely related idea to lives is health. With health, a character may take several hits until it is beaten or weakened.

Imagine that you want to insert a super strong brick into the game. You wouldn't want the player to break the super strong brick with one hit of the ball, right? That wouldn't be super strong.

With a bit of programming, you can track the number of hits a particular brick takes. Thus, you can now break the brick only when the number of hits crosses a threshold; or, you can weaken the brick by making it smaller with each subsequent hit.

Take a shot at building a super strong brick in the game that takes repeated hits to break. In the current design, you can place the brick above or below the current rows.

Adding more bricks to the level with a custom block

Currently, we have two rows of yellow bricks. Our next task will be to create a new brick color and add two more rows to the game using this new brick color. However, this will require us to revise our existing code that redraws the bricks, and through this revision, we will turn the current script into a custom block, which is a new feature in Scratch 2.0.

Time for action – creating a second brick

There are a couple of different ways to create a new brick color in the game. We can create a new sprite with the color or we can add a costume color to the existing brick sprite. This exercise will take the costume approach so that we can use a single custom block to draw all the rows and colors. The steps are as follows:

1. Let's ensure the brick has a valid name that will represent our changes. I recommend that you use the name brick instead of yellow brick.

2. From the **Costumes** tab of brick, add a new costume by using the **paint new costume** icon.

3. When the blank canvas of the paint editor opens, convert the image to vector and draw a solid red rectangle that is 45 pixels long and 25 pixels tall because that's how big the yellow bricks were. We did this exercise in *Chapter 6, Making an Arcade Game – Breakout (Part I)*.

To give you more control and make it easier to draw the image to a specific size, zoom in on the image using the zoom icon, as shown in the following screenshot:

4. After you draw the second costume, rename the costumes according to their color; for example, yellow and red.

Creating these bricks is the kind of process that could very well drive you mad. If you have problems, go get the book's code bundle and grab the same from the chapter code file. Also, note that the paint editor has a **Clear** button. You can use it to start over.

While resizing the sprites, try drawing the sprite smaller than you need it to be intentionally. Then, drag the edges of the sprite until it is the right size.

What just happened?

This exercise mirrors our efforts in *Chapter 6, Making an Arcade Game – Breakout (Part I)*. However, we now have a single brick sprite that has multiple colors, which we'll use in the game.

Time for action – drawing rows of bricks with custom blocks

The script to create the two rows of yellow bricks is working well; however, we're about to duplicate a lot of code and potentially have a really large and a difficult-to-manage script.

Let's break the duplicate code into a procedure, also known as a custom block in Scratch 2.0, as described in the following steps:

1. From the **Scripts** tab of the brick, click on the **More Blocks** palette and click on the **Make a Block** button.

2. In the **New Block** dialog that opens, type in `lay bricks` in the text field of the purple block and then click on **OK** to create the block.

3. After you create the block, Scratch places a block with the name **lay bricks** in the **More Blocks** palette, and in the **scripts** area, you now have a block titled **define lay bricks**.

4. If you look closely at the code to create the bricks, you'll note that everything in the **repeat** blocks is an exact duplicate. Break the script apart and attach one of the **repeat** blocks to **define lay bricks**.

5. Discard the other **repeat** block. We don't need it any more.

6. To ensure we're on the right track, let's get our script back to the state where it makes two rows of yellow bricks. Attach a **lay bricks** block to the first **go to x: () y: ()** block.

7. Then, add the second **go to x: () y: ()** block followed by another **lay bricks** block. Finish the stack by reattaching the **hide** block. The following screenshot shows our revised script alongside our old script:

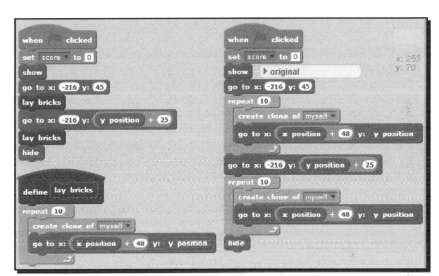

The preceding screenshot is only for illustration purposes. Running both of these scripts at the same time will produce wrong results.

8. If you haven't already tested the code, click on the green flag to ensure it still works.

9. Now, let's add the red brick. Detach the **hide** block for a few steps. Add a **switch costume to ()** block to the stack and select **red**.

10. Attach a duplicate of the **go to x: (-216) y: ((y position) + (25))** block, followed by a **lay bricks** block.

11. Repeat the previous step and reattach the **hide** block. Refer to the following screenshot for our new script.

12. Add a **switch costume to ()** block after the **show** block at the top of this script and choose **yellow**.

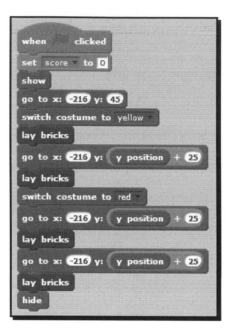

To delete a custom block, you must first remove all instances of the custom block from the scripts area. Then, you can drag the **define** block to the blocks palette to remove the custom block.

What just happened?

Have you ever built a fort in the backyard, a snow castle, or a LEGO house? If so, this process should look familiar. First, build a layer of a wall. Then, go to the top of the layer and add a new one. It's a repetitive process where you repeat steps until you're finished or tired.

As Scratch programmers, the repetition of code is a real pain. Note that in the first version of the script, we were required to duplicate all the code in the **repeat** block, two times for each brick color we add to the game. By refactoring our code to use a custom block, we've made the script easier to build, read, and maintain. Note that I'm not saying all duplication is bad or can be avoided, as we've clearly duplicated small snippets of blocks in previous exercises. However, duplicating two blocks, for example, is much more manageable than duplicating ten.

Now, for example, if we decide to change the width of the bricks, we have one place where we can make the change—in the **define lay bricks** stack.

I can hear you pointing out the obvious. "But Mike," you're saying, "what's with all the duplicate go to blocks?". Good point. We'll come back to that.

Introducing procedures by way of custom blocks

Procedures allow us to give a stack of blocks a name that can then be reused in other scripts, which avoids duplication. If you check out other languages, you may come across the term method or function.

The power custom blocks can be seen in the previous exercise. It's a consolidation of code in a single line or block.

 In Scratch 2.0, a custom block is only available to the sprite that you create it for, which is the sprite with the **define** block.

Prior to Scratch 2.0, Scratch programmers could use broadcasts as a way to provide some script deduplication. There are some obvious differences as you use custom blocks and broadcasts. For example, custom blocks accept inputs, whereas broadcasts do not support inputs (arguments). One of the less obvious differences is that the custom blocks can support recursion, which means the define stack can use the custom block as part of the procedure.

Setting custom block inputs

When we created the custom block in our exercise, you may have observed the **New Block** dialog had an **Options** menu. The options include **Add number input**, **Add string input**, **Add boolean input**, **Add label text**, and **Run without screen refresh**, as shown in the following screenshot:

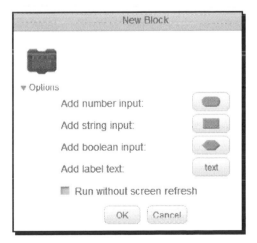

In the *Have a go hero – creating a custom block with options* exercise that follows, you'll have a chance to explore the custom block inputs. We'll also use custom block inputs in *Chapter 9, Turning Geometric Patterns into Art Using the Pen Tool*. The following table provides an overview and a sample of each custom block option:

Option	Description	Sample usage
Add number input	This option passes a number to the custom block definition. The code blocks in the sample usage column will shake the sprite six times.	
Add string input	With this option, the text that gets passed to the custom block definition can be printed via the block. In the sample usage code shown in the screenshot (on the right hand-side of this table), the block is passing a variable with a value 5 and the text Earthquake. When the block runs, the sprite will shake five times and then say **Earthquake**.	

Option	Description	Sample usage
Add boolean input	With this option, the statement is evaluated and runs the custom block if true.	
	The sample usage screenshot (on the right-hand side of this table) shows a block that evaluates whether or not the current costume equals 1. If the costume is 1, the sprite will shake 10 times.	
Add label text	This option will provide a block label that can give some context to the type of value that should be passed to the custom block.	In the string input example, **times and say** is the label on the block.
Run without screen refresh	If this option is checked, the block runs all at once rather than waiting between blocks.	This block can be used for very large calculations or scripts.

Have a go hero – creating a custom block with options

We demonstrated the power of procedures by way of custom blocks as a way to consolidate the code, but the current script to create the rows of bricks still has a lot of duplication.

Here's a two-part challenge. Pass the height of the brick costumes to the custom block, and incorporate the **go to x: -216 y: ((y position)+ (25))** calculation as part of the **lay bricks** procedure. You'll only need to pass the height of the brick because the procedure we created already accounts for the width of the brick in the **go to** block in the procedure. Even though the height value can always be 25 to match the actual height of our brick, we can change the height to be bigger than our current brick size, which would create white space between each row.

> You can edit the procedure and add options by right-clicking on the **define** block or the block name in the **More Blocks** palette.

Part two is to consolidate the script even further by passing the number of brick costumes you want to use as an input option to the procedure. By adding this input to the procedure, you have the necessary variables to make the procedure perform the entire work of building two rows of bricks for each costume.

The following screenshot shows a modified **lay bricks** block that passes the number of brick costumes and the height of the brick or height of row into the procedure. This stack successfully builds two yellow bricks and two rows of red bricks, just as we left off in our previous exercise. However, it uses considerably less blocks.

Need a hint? You need to have a control for three values: total costumes, row width, and two rows per costume. We have already built the procedure to handle two rows for one costume, so don't throw out what we've done.

Time for action – coordinating the ball play

Now that we have the rows of bricks built and we know all about custom blocks, it's time for an easier problem. In our script, the ball starts before the bricks are built. We can use broadcasts to coordinate the two events. The steps are as follows:

1. With the brick sprite selected, add a **broadcast** block to the end of the stack that builds the rows of bricks. Give it a clear name, such as `play`.

2. On the ball sprite, find the **forever** block with the **move (10) steps** and **if on edge, bounce** blocks.

3. Replace the **when flag clicked** block with the **when I receive** block. Select the **play** message.

4. Now, when you start the game, the ball should not start until after the bricks are all created. However, the ball remains visible on the screen. We must hide it by adding a **hide** block to the script that initializes the lives variable and sets the starting position and direction. Then, add a **show** block to the **when I receive (play)** block.

What just happened?

We don't want the game to start before the screen is fully set up. So, this exercise was all about getting our timing right by using the **broadcast** block to ensure the ball doesn't go into play while the game setup is still placing the bricks on the screen.

Have you noticed a trend yet? One change introduces another problem, which requires another incremental change. This iterative revision process occurs with any creative endeavor. Enjoy it.

Increasing ball speed and difficulty

At the moment, the ball is moving at a leisurely pace. We know by now that the higher the value we assign to the move block, the faster the ball goes.

Time for action – increasing ball speed

There are several criteria that we could use to increase the ball speed, such as score or number of hits. However, we're going to increase the ball speed based on the duration of the game. The steps are as follows:

1. To manipulate the ball speed as the script runs, we'll need a variable. So, create a variable named speed for the ball.

2. Find the ball script that begins with **when I receive (play)** and add a **set () to ()** block from the **Data** palette at the top of the stack. Select the **speed** variable and give it a starting value of 5.

3. From the **Sensing** palette, add a **reset timer** block. We'll use this block with the understanding that we won't use **reset timer** anywhere else in the project.

4. Inside the **forever** block, add an **if () then** block.

5. We're going to evaluate whether or not the **timer** block is greater than 10 by snapping the **() > ()** block from the **Operators** palette into the **if ()** block. Then, we will add the **timer** block from the **Sensing** palette into the first value. Type in 10 into the second value.

6. Inside the **if (timer > 10) then** block, add a **change () by** block. Select the speed variable and add a **multiplication** block from the **Operators** palette to the value. Multiply the speed variable by 1.2.

7. Add a **reset timer** block to the **if** block.

8. Finally, add the **speed reporter** block from the **Data** palette to the value of the **move** block.

9. Your script should look like the following screenshot. Play the game.

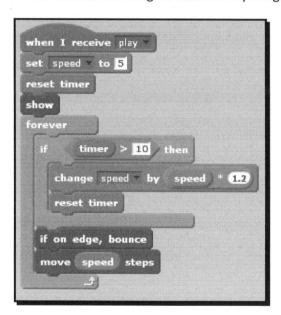

What just happened?

For every 10 seconds the player stays alive, the ball speed will increase by a factor of 1.2, which ensures we steadily increase the speed and progressively make the game harder. This project introduced the **timer** block, and if you enable the **timer reporter** block, you'll notice that the built-in time continually runs. By resetting it in our script, we have an easy way to count time intervals. Using more than one **reset timer** block in a project will have unintended consequences and create bugs.

There are three key adjustments in the script we just created: the starting value of the `speed` variable, the timer duration that we evaluate, and the multiplier value in the **change () by ()** block. This won't be the only difficulty that we will add to our game, but you can adjust these settings to get just the right ball speed.

Using Boolean evaluations

In Scratch, the Boolean blocks are hexagonal in shape and fit into the hexagonal values of other blocks. When a Boolean block is evaluated, it reports either `true` or `false`. Our previous exercise demonstrated a common way to control a script using the **Control** block and a Boolean evaluation. The Boolean evaluation, that is, **speed > 10** will either be `true` or `false`. If it's `true`, then the script increases the speed and the **reset the timer** block will run.

The following table shows the Boolean blocks included with Scratch:

Block	Location	Description
() < ()	Operators	This block returns `true` if the first value is less than the second value. It also compares the text (for example, a < b).
() = ()	Operators	This block returns `true` if the two values are equal. It also compares the text (for example, f = f).
() > ()	Operators	This block returns `truc` if the first value is greater than the second value. It also compares the text (for example, z > a).
() and ()	Operators	This block combines two Boolean blocks where both have to be `true` to report true.
() or ()	Operators	This block combines two Boolean blocks but only one of them has to be `true` in order to report true.
not ()	Operators	This block evaluates the Boolean to see whether it is `false` and reports `true` if the condition is `false`; likewise, it reports `talse` if the condition is `true`.
touching ()?	Sensing	This block reports `true` if the current sprite is touching the specified sprite.
touching color ()?	Sensing	This block reports `true` if the current sprite is touching the specified color.
color () is touching ()?	Sensing	This block reports `true` if the specified sprite color is touching the specified color of the stage or any other sprite.
mouse down ()?	Sensing	This block reports `true` if the left mouse button is clicked.

Block	Location	Description
key () pressed?	**Sensing**	This block reports `true` if the specified key is pressed.
sensor ()?	**Sensing**	This block is only available for use with a PicoBoard. It reports `true` if the specified button is pressed or the specified port is connected.
() contains ()	**Data**	This block reports `true` if the specified list contains the specified text. This block only shows up when a list is created.

All programming languages will use Boolean expressions, comparisons, and conditional statements as fundamental ways to control what happens in the program.

Keeping score based on a clone's costume

Our Breakout game deserves another challenge. This time, we're going to keep track of the costume number of the cloned bricks so that we can decrease the paddle size when some of the yellow bricks are broken.

Time for action – decreasing the paddle size based on the clones' costume

We have three main tasks. We need to create a smaller costume for the paddle, create the script to keep track of how many times the ball touches the brick's yellow costume, and then build the script that changes the paddle's costume.

To detect the yellow costume of the brick, we have multiple solutions available to us. However, we're going to pick a slightly more complicated solution because it offers us more flexibility for future enhancements. We'll revisit some alternatives after we work through the exercise. The steps are as follows:

1. Let's start with the paddle first. Duplicate the existing paddle costume and then use the eraser tool to make the costume smaller. Let's name the costumes something meaningful, such as **big** and **small**.

2. While we're thinking about it, let's ensure our game always starts with the big paddle costume visible. Create a **when flag clicked** stack for the paddle and add the **switch costume to (big)** block.

3. Now, we need to keep track of how many times the ball hits the yellow sprite's costumes. To do this, we're going to assign a unique ID number to each clone. For the ball, create a variable named `clone id` and set it to **For this sprite only**.

4. In the **define lay bricks** stack, add a **change (clone id) by (1)** block before the **create clone of (myself)** block.

5. Remember, any time we manipulate a variable or setting, we need to reset the value at the start of the game. Add a **set (clone id) to (0)** block to the **when flag clicked** stack that builds the rows of bricks. The following screenshot shows the modifications to the brick sprite's scripts. Your stacks may be slightly different if you did the hero exercise earlier in this chapter.

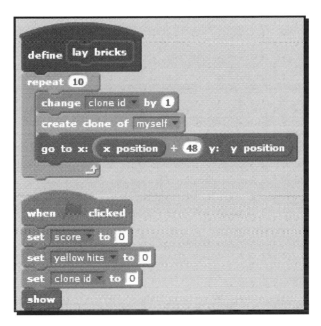

6. Now that each clone has an ID, we need to evaluate that ID when the ball touches the clone to determine if we count the hit. To track the hits to the yellow bricks, create a variable named **yellow hits** and set it to **For all sprites**.

7. When Scratch creates a clone of the sprite, the clone inherits the variables assigned to the sprite. If the variable is local to the sprite, it becomes local to the instance of the clone and will only be accessible to the clone. However, a global variable will be available to all clones. Add an **if () then** block to the **if (touching ((ball)?) then** conditional statement in the **when I start as a clone** stack and evaluate the **((clone id) < (21))** statement.

8. Add a **change () by ()** block to the **if (clone id) < 21) then** statement. Select the **yellow hits** variable and enter 1 for the change by value. The following screenshot shows the script:

9. Now, we need to tell the paddle to shrink, so select the paddle sprite. Start a new stack with the **when I receive (play)** block. Add an **if () then** block.

10. In the **if** block, evaluate **if yellow hits = 0**.

11. Inside the **if ((yellow hits) = (10)) then** block, add the **switch costume to ()** block and select **small**.

12. After the **change (yellow hits) by ()** block and evaluate the **((yellow hits) = (10))** statement.

What just happened?

The challenge of this exercise is detecting the costume of another sprite, or in this case, a clone. Scratch does not provide us with a touching **(costume #) of (sprite)** block. This block would have alleviated a lot of code. Instead, we had to get creative.

By assigning the clone a unique ID number at the time the clone is created, we can track that clone no matter where it is on the stage. This is just like the GPS signal from your smart phone that can be used to locate your position anywhere in the world among millions of similar devices. Cloning the costumes of the bricks is a systematic process, and we've already defined the math behind that process. Each costume gets cloned 10 times per row for two rows. That's a total of 20 cloned bricks per costume.

This means the yellow bricks are represented by clone IDs 1 through 20. The red bricks can be identified by clone IDs 21 through 40. This gives us the first Boolean evaluation, that is, **if ((clone id) < 21))**.

If the clone ID is less than 21, we instruct the script to add 1 to the yellow hits variable. Then, the paddle continually checks to see whether yellow hits equals 10. When it does, the paddle switches to the small costume, thereby creating a more challenging game.

If you followed my step-by-step instructions, then your game should work. However, if you doubted the reason to make the **yellow hits** variable global and instead opted to choose **For this sprite only**, then you have a broken script at the moment. If you make yellow hits a local (**For this sprite only**) variable, then the **change (yellow hits) by (1)** variable will not increment. This is because all clones can access a global variable; however, the **For this sprite only** variables are assigned to individual clones, which means the brick clones would not be able to access the **yellow hits** variable of the parent sprite unless it is created for all sprites.

In the game, shrinking the paddle after ten yellow bricks are broken does not mean that no red bricks were broken. You can opt to shrink the paddle after 10 bricks of any color. As a game designer, determining how hard you make the game and at what point you add a challenge is your privilege.

Considering alternative solutions

Here's another way to solve the problem of tracking the hits to the yellow bricks. In the following screenshot, the script checks the costume number to determine when to increment the **yellow hits** variable. All the yellow bricks have a costume equal to 1 and all the red bricks have a costume equal to 2.

This would be a really good simple solution. However, it's limiting in that we have 20 instances of costume 1 displaying on the stage. What if we wanted to single out the tenth yellow brick? Looking for costume 1 is not going to help us.

Next, consider the following screenshot, which shows that we can use the **() and ()** block to ensure that the hit only counts the updated **yellow hits** variable if the ball is touching the brick and the color of the brick is yellow:

The code in the previous screenshots would eliminate a variable and the step of assigning a unique clone ID.

The clone IDs give us more flexibility for future features precisely because we can identify each clone individually. By using the clone ID, we can assign weighted points to each brick, which affects the game score, or we can count the number of total bricks broken as a way to detect when the level is clear.

The point is that no perfect solution exists, so we roll with the best one that meets our needs and abilities at the time.

Time for action – detecting when we clear the level

How do we know when the level is over? The answer is simple, that is, when all the bricks are broken; so, let's build the simple answer. We know that at the start of the game, there are 40 bricks on the screen. Let's follow the given steps to detect when we clear the level:

1. The **cloud id** variable has a record of the total number of bricks we built. Let's assign that value to a new variable named **level hits**. Then, we'll actually count down the **level hits** variable with each broken brick.

2. Select the **brick** sprite. Add the **set () to ()** block to the end of the stack that uses the **lay brick** custom block. Select **level hits** as the variable and drag the **cloud id** reporter block from the **Data** palette to the **to** value. Check your blocks against the following screenshot:

3. Each time the ball breaks a brick, we will reduce the value in the **level hits** variable. Add a **change (level hits) by (-1)** block after the **change (score) by (1)** block in the **when I start as a clone** stack.

4. Finally, we need to stop the ball when the **level hits** variable is equal to zero. Add an **if () then** block after the **change (level hits) by (-1)** block. Then, add the **condition (level hits) = (0)** block.

5. Add a **broadcast** block to the **if ((level hits) = (0)) then** block. Create a new message named **level clear**. The following screenshot shows the revised script:

6. To the ball, add a new script that starts with a **when I receive (level clear)** block.

7. Then, add a **hide** block.

What just happened?

We now have a way to stop our game after the player successfully clears the level. Stopping the game at this point really means we stop the ball by hiding it. We didn't use the **stop (all)** block because you may want to add a second level and the **stop (all)** block will not allow to continue with the project.

No matter how many bricks we place on the screen, our script will always know when all the bricks have been broken by using the clone ID value to provide the total number of bricks on the stage.

Keeping the score using cloud variables

We'll wrap this chapter up with a small script to assign the player's score to a high score variable that we will store in the **cloud**. Consider this a value-added feature because you could stop right now and have a fully functional game. Depending on your privacy concerns, you may not wish to record information to the cloud, which will include the user name, score, and access time. The cloud refers to storing information on an internet-based server, which is hosted by the Scratch Team in this case.

Time for action – keeping a global scoreboard

Currently, there are two conditions in our script that signify the end of the game. The first is when the player clears the level. The second is when the player's lives become zero. Because we have some duplication, we'll use a custom block to set the score. The steps are as follows:

1. With the ball sprite selected, select the **More Blocks** palette and click on the **Make a block** button to create a block named **update scoreboard**.

2. Add the **scoreboard** block to the **when I receive (level clear)** block.

3. Add the **scoreboard** block before the **stop (all)** script in the **if ((lives) = (0)) then** block.

4. We need to add a new cloud variable to use in the **define update scoreboard** block. From the **Data** palette, click on the **Make a variable** button. Name the variable scoreboard and select the cloud variable (stored on the server) checkbox.

5. When you click on **OK** to create the project's first cloud variable, you will get an information box that tells you the cloud variables can only be numbers. You can click on this message to clear it.

6. Add a **set () to ()** block to the **define update scoreboard** block. Select **scoreboard** as the variable and add the **score reporter** block to the **to** value. The following screenshot shows the changes we just made to the scripts for the ball:

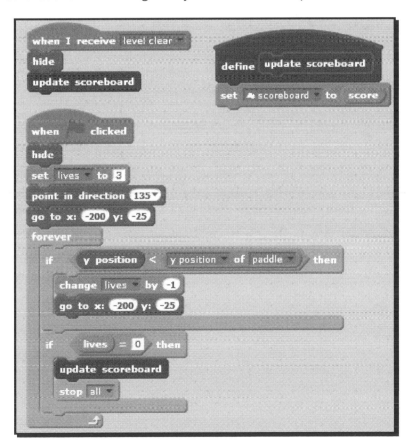

What just happened?

By using a Scratch 2.0 feature called cloud variables, we created a scoreboard that gets stored on the Scratch website. It can only be accessed by our game, but everybody who plays the game can potentially record their score in the cloud.

If you decide to add a second level to this game, then you will need to remove the custom scoreboard block from the **when I receive (level clear)** block and add it to the new last level.

Understanding cloud variables in Scratch 2.0

Being able to store data in the cloud that all users of a Scratch project can access alludes to great programming possibilities. In the current implementation of Scratch 2.0, cloud variables' main benefit is the ability to track high scores in games and to conduct surveys because of the limitations the Scratch Team has placed on their use. As the exercise pointed out, cloud variables are limited to numbers.

Cloud variables are only available to users who are signed into their Scratch account; however, not all Scratch users can access cloud data. New users will most certainly not be able to access cloud data. According to the cloud data FAQ by the Scratch Team, users must achieve a Scratcher status before being able to access the cloud. How one attains the Scratcher status is ambiguously described by the Scratch Team as follows:

> You can become a Scratcher through actively participating on the website.

The FAQ section has more information at `http://scratch.mit.edu/help/faq/#clouddata`.

These limitations are in place as of early 2014. As Scratch 2.0 matures, I would expect the cloud data features to evolve and become more flexible.

Viewing the cloud data log

After you share a project with the world and the users start interacting with it, the cloud data is written to the Scratch website (that is, the server). When another user remixes a project, the new project has its own cloud data. The signed-in users can see it by viewing the project page on the website and clicking on **Cloud Data Log**.

The following screenshot shows the kind of information displayed when a user is logged on to the server:

Oreo survey: Cookie or Creme? » Cloud data history

User	Data Name	Action	Data Value	Time
	creme-votes	set_var	103	1 week ago
	creme-votes	set_var	102	1 month, 2 weeks ago
	creme-votes	set_var	101	1 month, 2 weeks ago
	creme-votes	set_var	100	1 month, 3 weeks ago

As you can see, the user, the information about the data, and the access time are all recorded and are publicly available.

Pop quiz – reviewing the chapter's concepts

Q1. A custom block can be used by:

1. All sprites in the project.
2. All sprites with a global variable.
3. Only scripts that use a Boolean value.
4. Only the sprite it was created for.

Q2. A Boolean reports:

1. The value of the variable.
2. Either true or false the high score of the game.
3. A comparison of two numbers using the and operator.
4. None of these.

Q3. When using variables with clones, you should make the variable:

1. For all sprites.
2. For this sprite only.
3. A cloud variable.
4. Clones can't access variables.

Q4. A cloud variable enables a project to:

1. Pass data from one sprite to another sprite.
2. Consolidate duplicate code into a single script.
3. Simulate a sky theme.
4. Store variable data on the Scratch server.

Have a go hero – extending Breakout

There are a many ways you could improve and extend this project based on the foundation we've built in the last two chapters. Here are several things to do: add a second level, add more levels of bricks, design a welcome screen, and calculate a score bonus.

Summary

We finished this chapter with a technically sound framework for a Breakout game that introduces a couple of Scratch 2.0's highly touted features—custom blocks and cloud variables. Of course, the concepts we've used in this chapter can be combined with everything we've learned so far to create an entirely different game of your own design.

In the next chapter, we'll create a snarky fortune teller to help answer all our questions. The project will prompt the player for a question and the all-knowing psychic will provide an answer. In the process, we'll introduce lists to store groups of data and work on scanning text strings.

8
Chatting with a Fortune Teller

In the Breakout game we created in the previous chapters, we learned how easy it is to create projects that keep track of the changing values by using variables. However, variables have a limitation in they store only one value at a time. In this chapter, we're going to create a random fortune-spewing teller, which will require the sprites to have access to a list of multiple values at one time.

Welcome to lists. In Scratch, a list feature allows us to associate one list with multiple items or values in almost the same way we create a list before going to the grocery store. We can think of the items in the list as variables. Each list item can be changed, removed, or added to.

In this chapter, we will take a trip to the fortune teller to demonstrate lists, and I am sure you'll learn how to:

- ◆ Store and retrieve information in lists
- ◆ Prompt the player for project inputs, check for errors, and identify patterns with the mod block
- ◆ Use the **if () then else** block to control the program
- ◆ Develop a project test plan
- ◆ Create a keyword scanner to split and identify words and letters

Creating, importing, and exporting lists

Most of us enjoy a good circus, carnival, or county fair. There's fun, food, and fortunes. What would a fair be without the fortune teller tent? By the end of the chapter, you'll know everything you need to spin your own fortunes and amaze your friends with your wisdom.

Time for action – creating lists to store multiple values

Before we start the first exercise, create a new project with exactly two sprites. The first sprite will be the seeker. The second sprite will be the teller. Choose any sprites you want and edit them in any way you wish. My seeker will be **Pico** and my teller will be a **Wizard**, both from Scratch's image library. The seeker will ask the questions and the teller will provide the fortune or the answers to the seeker's questions. As you import your sprites, name them seeker and teller because that is how I'll refer to them throughout the rest of the chapter.

In order to have a successful fortune telling session, we need two things: a question and an answer. Let's start by defining some questions and answers as given in the following steps:

1. Select the **seeker** from the list of sprites.
2. From the **Data** palette, click on the **Make a List** button.
3. In the **list name** dialog box, type in questions and select **For all sprites**.
4. Click on **OK** to create the list. Several new blocks will be displayed in the **Variables** palette, and a stage monitor titled **questions** displays on the stage.

5. Think about a couple of questions you may be tempted to ask; for example, "Are you a real physic?" or "If a tree falls in the woods, will it make a sound?".

6. Let's add our proposed questions to the **questions** list. Click on the plus sign (+) located at the bottom-left corner of the **questions** stage monitor (on the stage) to add an item to list; a text input field will be displayed. If Scratch populates your text box with *****, remove them and then type in your first question.

7. Click on the plus sign (+) again and enter the second question. We now have two questions in our list.

8. Let's add a **say () for () secs** block to the scripts area of the **seeker** sprite so we can start the dialog.

9. From the **Data** palette, drag the **item (1) of (questions)** block to the text value of the **say() for () secs** block.

10. Click on the block for the seeker to ask the first question in the list.

11. Change the position value on the **item** block to **last** and click on the block again. This time the seeker asks the second question, which is also the last question.

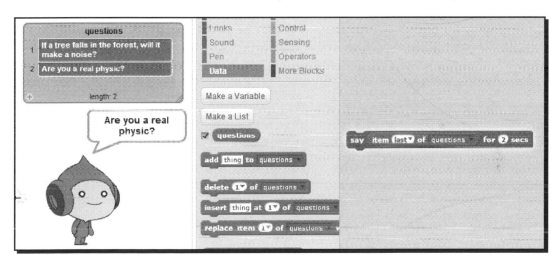

What just happened?

I'm certain you could come up with a hundred different questions to ask a fortune teller. Don't worry; you'll get your chance to ask more questions later.

Our exercise introduced another group of **Data** blocks that allow us to work with lists. Like variables, making a new list makes several new **Data** blocks available. The new list contains zero items, and as we saw in the exercise, we can add items directly to the list.

Another similarity with the variables is that the scope of the list can be limited to **this sprite only** or extended to all sprites. We chose to make the questions list for all sprites because we will want the teller to access the list of seeker questions later.

 If you work with other programming languages, then you will likely refer to the lists as arrays.

A quick way to access the items in the list was with the **item () of ()** block. In our example, we accessed two items in the list: **1** and **last**. This value was passed to the **say** block so we saw it being displayed on the screen.

The most notable difference between lists and variables is that lists can contain multiple items, and therefore, multiple values which are accessible via a numbered index. It's a lot like creating a to-do list.

Working with an item in a list

We can use lists to group related items, but accessing the items in the list requires an extra level of specificity.

 To access an item in a list, we need to know the list name and the position of the item in the list. In Scratch, the first item of the list is made available by using the number one. In other programming languages, however, the first item may be accessed via the number zero.

The following table shows the available ways to interact with the items in a list and the associated blocks:

Position	Description	Use and blocks
1	This position identifies the first item in the list	It is found in the following blocks: ◆ **delete () of ()** ◆ **insert () of ()** ◆ **replace item () of ()**
random	This position selects a random item from the list	It is found in the following blocks: ◆ **insert () of ()** ◆ **replace item () of ()**
last	This position selects the last item in the list	It is found in the following blocks: ◆ **delete () of ()** ◆ **insert () of ()** ◆ **replace item () of ()**
all	This position selects all items in the list for deletion	It is found in the following blocks: ◆ **delete () of ()**
reporter	This option reports all the items in the list as a string	The most common use is to show the list monitor on the stage by clicking on the checkbox next to the block's name in the **Data** palette
Specify an item number	This option enters a specific item number	Type in a number, such as 3, to access the third item in the list

Importing a list

Entering one item at a time via the Scratch interface is functional, but the small size of the list monitor can be difficult to use when you need to add a large number of items. Fortunately, there's an easier way. You can create a text file outside of Scratch and then import it to your list.

Time for action – importing fortunes to a list

Now, we'll see how easy it is to import an existing text file to a Scratch list called **answers**. You can use any answers you want, but I'm going to use a list of the common Magic 8-Ball responses available via Wikipedia at http://en.wikipedia.org/wiki/Magic_8_ball. My list will contain 20 answers to start.

Let's follow the given steps for importing fortunes to a list:

1. Create a new list for the teller called `answers`.

2. Build a plain text file with the answers you want to use in response to the seeker's questions. Enter one answer per line in a plain text editor. The following screenshot shows my list of answers. The book's source files will include a sample `answers.txt` file.

3. To import the list, right-click on the **answers** list monitor and choose **import**. This will erase any items you previously added to the **answers** list.

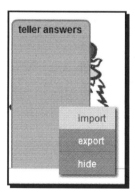

4. In the **Import List** dialog box, browse to the answers text file you saved on your computer prior to starting this exercise and select it. The **answers** list in Scratch now contains the contents of the text file.

What just happened?

I don't know about you, but I had a much easier time typing in a text editor than I did typing in the list monitor that gets created on the Scratch stage. Actually, if you took my lead, you copied the Magic 8-Ball responses from Wikipedia and pasted them into a text file. That way, the only typing you had to do was to clean up some formatting.

If you completed the cloud variable exercise in *Chapter 7, Programming a Challenging Gameplay – Breakout (Part II)*, you might be thinking that creating a cloud list would be a good feature. As of early January 2014, Scratch does not include the cloud functionality for lists. The early alpha versions of Scratch 2.0 did include references to cloud lists, so it's reasonable to expect that a future release will put lists in the cloud.

Exporting a list from Scratch

As you create your projects, the contents of a list may change. In that case, you may want to export the new list, or as a game designer, you may want to export a backup of the list so that you could revert to a saved copy, because after an item is removed from the list, it cannot be recovered.

To export a list, right-click on the **list** monitor and click on **export**.

Exporting and importing a list has one big limitation. There are no Scratch blocks to either import or export a list.

Prompting the player for a question

If we wanted to have the seeker and teller interact independently of the player, then the two lists we have would accomplish that. We could randomly pull a question from the seeker's list and then match it up to a response from the teller's list. Our game, however, is going to be more interactive than that.

By using Scratch's **ask () and wait** block, the teller can prompt the player for a question on behalf of the seeker. In other words, the seeker sprite will represent the human player.

Let's take a look at an example.

Time for action – asking a question

Our task is to make the seeker have a conversation with the teller and ultimately, ask a question. Select the **seeker** sprite, and let's begin:

1. First, clean the clutter from the stage. Right-click on each of the list monitors and select **hide**.

2. Let's stitch together some dialog between the two sprites. From the **Events** palette, add the **when this sprite clicked** block to the **scripts** area.

3. Attach a **say () for () secs** block and change the text value to a pleasant introductory sentence such as Hi, wise teller. Do you have my fortune?.

4. Add a **broadcast ()** block, and create a new message named intro (short for introduction) as a way to signal the teller that the seeker is ready, as shown in the following screenshot:

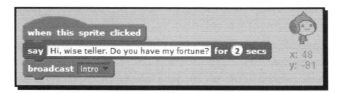

5. For the teller, add a **when I receive (intro)** block to the **scripts** area, and attach an **ask () and wait** block from the **Sensing** palette. Replace the text value of the **ask** block with something that prompts the player to ask a question on behalf of the seeker, such as What would you like to know?.

6. After the teller receives the question, add a **broadcast ()** block and create a new messaged named fortune. Refer to the following screenshot for the teller's script:

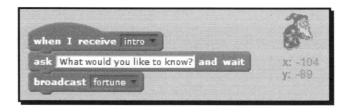

7. At this point, if you click on the **seeker**, you should be prompted for the question. You can type in a question in the text box provided and then press *Enter*. Pressing *Enter* saves the text you typed to the **answer** block, which is located in the **Sensing** palette. The following screenshot shows the teller prompting the seeker for the question:

8. Let's add the question to the question list when the seeker receives the fortune broadcast. Select the **seeker** sprite and add the **add () to ()** block from the **Data** palette to a **when I receive (fortune)** block from the **Events** palette. From the **Sensing** palette, drag the **answer** block to the first value. Select **questions** for the second value.

9. As a debug step to verify whether the question was properly stored, add the following block to the seeker's **when I receive (fortune)** stack: **say (item (last) of (questions)) for (1) secs**. The following screenshot shows both the scripts we created for the seeker. You can remove the **say** block after you do the verifications.

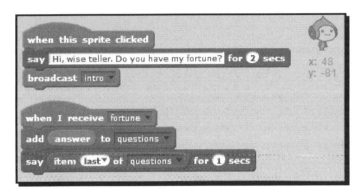

What just happened?

Coordinating the back and forth conversation between the seeker and the teller by using the **broadcast ()** blocks should be second nature to you by now. In our fortune teller game, the player is the seeker, so the **ask () and wait** block prompts you, the seeker, for a question. The **ask () and wait** block forces the script to wait for the keyboard input, which means our script stopped until we provided input.

We'll make the teller answer the question in an upcoming exercise, but for now, we've prompted the player for a question and saved that question to the questions lists via the **answer** block. By saving each question, the seeker has a growing list of questions.

Because the question list is for all sprites, we could have the teller add the item to the list. However, I've made a self-imposed decision that only the seeker will modify the questions list even though I want the teller to be able to see it—we are creating a fortune teller, after all. Also, by sending a broadcast, we provide a cue back to the seeker that a fortune is coming. This is an opportunity for future game enhancement by changing the seeker's reaction.

We can use the stored questions in a variety of ways. For example, we could script an automated demo of the game, or we could check for duplicate answers as a way to prevent sneaky seekers from repeating questions and uncovering the teller's deception.

Using stored questions

If we wanted to make the seeker repeat the question, the **say (answer) for (2) secs** block that we used as a verification step provides the way to access the last question in the list. In our game, we will use the list of stored questions as a way to check for duplicate questions from the player, which will allow us to add error checking into the game.

Time for action – validating the seeker's question

Now that we're prompting the player for a question via the seeker and adding it to the questions list, it is a good idea to check for some common errors that may come our way. First, we're going to make sure the seeker types something into the textbox when prompted. Secondly, we're going to check for the duplicate questions because receiving different answers for the same question may expose the teller's randomness.

Select the **Scripts** tab of the **teller** sprite and let's begin:

1. In the **when I receive (intro)** stack, add a **repeat () until** block right before the **broadcast (fortune)** block.

2. As we have two conditions to check, insert the **() and ()** block from the **Operators** palette to the value in the **repeat () until** block.

3. In the first value of the **and** block, add a greater than (>) block.

4. To the first value of the greater than block, add the **length of ()** block from the **Operators** palette. Then, add the **answer** block as the length value.

5. In the second value of the greater than block, type in a relatively small number, such as 5.

6. Now, let's build the second condition in the **and** block. From the **Operators** palette, add the **not ()** block. Then, add the **() contains ()** block from the **Data** palette. Select questions from the available lists. Add the **answer** block to the **contains** value.

7. The command that we want to repeat until both conditions evaluate as true is the **ask () and wait** block. Add the block and change the ask value to something appropriate, such as `Please ask your question`.

8. Test the script by running the program and don't forget to provide invalid answers. The following screenshot shows the revised script:

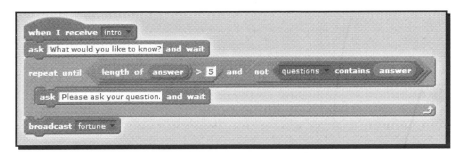

What just happened?

We just added a bit of error handling to our script by way of the **repeat () until** block. We first evaluated the answer to ensure that the length of the answer is more than five characters. This essentially creates a minimum length requirement for questions. In reality, I don't know of any question that can be asked in five characters, but having this condition provides a starting point for us. Feel free to make the minimum length more difficult by increasing the 5 value in the **length of (answer) > 5** block. A `false` value will cause the teller to prompt the seeker for a new question.

In the second condition, we check to see whether the seeker has asked the question before. The **() contains ()** block checks the value stored in the answer variable with each item in the **questions** lists. If it finds a match, it reports `true`. A **true** value will cause the teller to prompt the seeker for a new question because the **not** operator inverts `true` to `false`.

Only when both conditions are `true` do we allow the teller to respond with the fortune, which is signaled with the **broadcast (fortune)** block.

One of the limitations of this approach is that we can only detect exact matches between the **answer** value and the contents of the **questions** list. An extra space or a typo creates a different value.

Deleting the list values

As you spend time creating and testing the scripts, you may want to clear your **questions** list so that you can start with an empty list. Scratch has a block for that.

The **delete () of ()** block can be found in the **Data** palette. The first value of the block accepts a position in the list and the second value selects the list. You can specify a number, **1** or **all**. The following screenshot shows the full command to remove all the items from the questions list:

You could run the block manually to remove the list items or add it as part of the start up script when the green flag is clicked.

Have a go hero – finding and using the player's username

You want a smart and cordial fortune teller, right?

Scratch 2.0 introduced a new block in the **Sensing** palette called `username`, which reports the username of the player who is viewing the project. Modify the teller's initial response to address the player (also known as the seeker) by his or her username.

Remember that not all users will be signed into their Scratch account, or they may be using an offline version of Scratch, which means the username will not be available. Your script should check for the value of the username. How do you know if the player's **username** block has a value? Think about how we evaluated the length of the seeker's question.

Selecting a random fortune

The reason we visit the fortune teller is to hear a fortune. It's time to make the teller pull a random fortune just like real life.

Time for action – selecting a random fortune

We're going to use a separate stack of blocks to handle the script to issue a fortune. The steps are as follows:

1. With the **teller** sprite selected, add a **when I receive (fortune)** block to the scripts area. Attach a **say () for () secs** block.

2. From the **Data** palette, drag the **item () of ()** block into the first value of the **say** block. Select **random** for the position value and **answers** from the available lists.

3. Test the program by clicking on the **seeker** sprite. If all goes well, you will receive an answer (that is, a fortune) in response to your question. If your seeker repeats the question, you can remove the **say** block we used as a debug step in the previous exercise. The following screenshot shows our sample script so far.

What just happened?

We'll pause here for a brief moment, so you can reflect on your future life as a physic in the carnival. Our game framework is complete in that we have everything we need to ask a question and receive a fortune.

In this exercise, we reiterated our use of the **item () of ()** and **say** blocks. Based on our use of the **item () of ()** and **say** blocks, we can answer any question that can come our way, and our response will seem profound. At least, that's what we'll choose to believe.

Time for action – counting our fortunes with mod

Now, we will refine how the teller determines what fortune to give by counting the questions and issuing a negative response for every fifth question. If you copied the list of Magic 8-Ball responses, as I did, then your negative responses are items 15 through 20 in the **answers** list. If you added your own answers to the list, move the negative responses to the end of the list. You can do this in a text editor and reimport the **answers** list. The steps are as follows:

1. Our first task is to set up a variable to count how many questions the seeker asks so that we can calculate whether or not it's time to answer in negatives. Select the teller from the sprites list and create a new variable named question number and make it **For this sprite only**.

2. Add the **when flag clicked** block to the scripts area.

3. From the **Variables** palette, add the **set question number to (0)** block to the **when flag clicked** block. Now, we have a way to reset our counter at the start of the game. Refer to the following screenshot:

4. Next, we need to assign a value to the question number variable when the teller answers the seeker. We can do this by adding a **change (question number) by (1)** block to the end of the **when I receive (fortune)** script. Refer to the following screenshot:

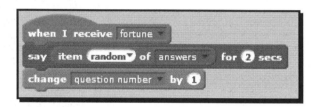

5. Our goal is to make the teller sprite give a range of answers based on the question number. From the **Control** palette, add the **if () then else** block to the **change (question number) by (1)** block.

6. Drag the **say ((item (random) of (answers)) for (2) secs** block to the "c" part of the **if () then else** block.

7. Add a **pick random () to ()** block to the position value of the **item () of ()** block, which replaces the block's random selection. Does it seem strange that we're replacing the block's built-in random value with a **pick random** block? If it does, the reason why we're doing this will be revealed soon.

8. Type in the number 15 to the first value of the **pick random** block. For the second value, add the **length of ()** block from the **Data** palette. Insert the **answers** block as the value.

9. Now, we need to supply a condition to the **if** block to test whether or not we should force a negative response. Add the equals to (=) block to the **if** block.

10. Drag the **() mod ()** block from the **Operators** palette to the first value.

11. We're going to use the **() mod ()** block to divide the **question number** variable by **5** so that we can calculate the remainder. Add the **question number** block to the first value of the **() mod ()** block.

The **() mod O ()** block reports the remainder of a division problem, which makes it useful to identify intervals with numbers.

12. Change the second value of the **() mod ()** block to **5** so the block reads **(question number) mod (5)**.

13. Test the script by seeking a fortune. With our current setup, the teller only responds on the fifth question, and it's always a negative response. Refer to the following screenshot:

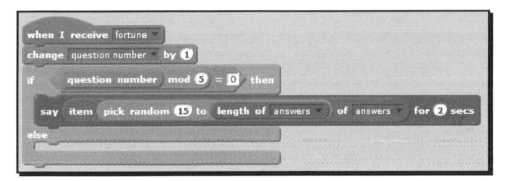

 If you display the question number stage monitor, you can display a slider by right-clicking on the stage monitor. The slider lets you assign a value to the variable, which can help you test your scripts, as shown in the following screenshot:

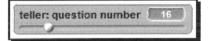

What just happened?

We asked our teller to only issue a negative response every fifth question, but we needed a way to let our teller sprite determine when the fifth question was asked. We created the **question number** variable as a counter to track the questions the seeker asked.

In our script, there are a couple of different ways to think about the question number. The variable is counting the number of fortunes received, which could be further qualified as the number of questions accepted by the teller. By incrementing the counter in the **when I receive (fortune)** stack of blocks, we ensure the seeker's question has passed the error checks we created.

The **() mod ()** block gave us the logic we needed to let the teller calculate whether or not to issue a negative response. The **() mod ()** block returns the remainder, which means our script is looking for a remainder of zero—in other words, if we divide a number by five and receive a remainder of zero, we know that the question being asked is an increment of 5 (for example, 5, 10, 15, 20, and so on). And when the remainder is zero, we pick a negative answer from the list. If we wanted to change the pattern to every fourth question, then the check would become **question number mod 4 = 0**.

Prior to this exercise, we used the default position value of random in the **item () of ()** block to select a random item from the list for the fortune. However, in our exercise, we wanted to restrict the range of possible fortunes, so we used the **pick random (15) to (length of (answers))** blocks. The **length of ()** block reports the current length of the list in terms of items. In my answers list, the length is 20; therefore, the calculation picks a random number between 15 and 20.

The else part of the **if () then else** block is empty, which is why the teller only issued a response on every fifth question. We'll build the rest of our script as we work through the remaining exercises.

Using magic numbers

In programming, one of the definitions of magic numbers is using constant values in your code when those values don't really have a clear meaning, and if you work on somebody else's code, you'll encounter this frequently. Someone's else hack is your pain.

Our expression that picks the negative answer fits the definition of a magic number because we're defining the range between 15 and the last item position in the list. When someone else edits this project, they're going to wonder why we chose this range. Additionally, it will be worse if someone else adds items to the answers list; that person won't know that the specified range has a purpose.

Do we have to fix this? At the very least, that section of code should be commented so that people have some understanding about what it accomplishes. One solution would be to move the negative responses to a new list. Then, we run the risk of maintaining duplicate answers across multiple lists, among some other potential problems. Another solution would be to use variables to set the start and end positions of our negative responses.

In the next exercise, we will fix our magic number and make our code clearer.

Creating a custom say fortune block

At this point, we have our teller that issues a negative fortune every fifth question, but we don't have any blocks in place to provide an answer to the rest of the questions. So, we'll fix that.

Time for action – creating a custom say fortune block

We're about to duplicate a script, so we're going to take this opportunity to create a custom block to select an item from the answers list based on a specified range of items.

1. With the teller sprite selected, click on the **Make a Block** button from the **More Blocks** palette. Name the block `say fortune in range:`. Then, add a number input and change the input name to `start range`. Next, add a label with the text **and**; finish the block by adding another number with the name `end range`. The following screenshot shows the resulting **define** block:

2. We want to use a similar set of blocks that we've already added to the **if () then else** block as we previously added to the **when I receive (fortune)** stack. The new expression will be **say (item (pick random start range) to (end range) of (possible answers)) for (2) secs**, as shown in the following screenshot:

3. Let's put the **custom** block to use in the **when I receive (fortune)** script. Find the **say () for ()** block that runs when the condition in the **if () then** block evaluates to `true` and replace it with a **say fortune in range: () and ()** block from the **More Blocks** palette.

4. Now, let's fix our magic number. Create two variables named `start neg resp` and `end neg resp`. They can be for this sprite (teller) only. Note that I'm abbreviating my names due to space constraints. Feel free to be verbose.

5. Add the **start neg resp** reporter block to the first value in the **say fortune** block and the **range () and ()** block. The **end neg resp** reporter block goes in the second value.

6. We can initialize the values of the new variables as part of the existing **when flag clicked** stack by setting the **start neg resp** variable to **15** and the **end neg resp** variable to **19**, or we can use the numbers that represent your range of negative answers.

7. Next, we need to have the teller predict a fortune when the question does not fit the pattern of every fifth question. The expression in the else part of the block is **say fortune in range: (1) and (length of (answers))**.

8. The following screenshot shows our revised scripts, including the initialization script:

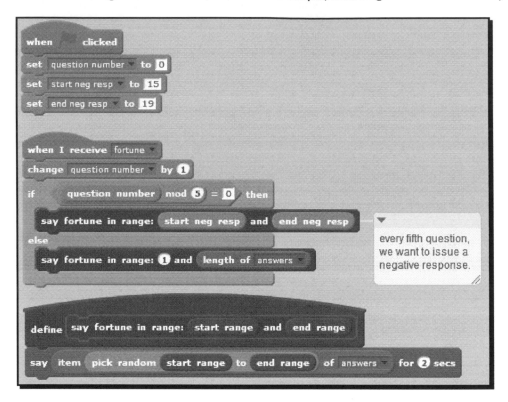

What just happened?

Blocks are cheap. Don't be afraid to throw your chosen blocks out in favor of something better.

In this exercise, we opted to create a custom block so that we can have more control over the range of answers the teller selects from. The scripts functionally achieve what we've already done; however, we avoided some duplication in the script as well as created a procedure that could be easily adapted and expanded upon.

Using the if () then else block

In earlier chapters, we've become familiar with the **if () then** block as a way to run a script when a condition is `true`. The `false` condition doesn't trigger any code.

In contrast, the **if () then else** control block evaluates a condition, and if the evaluation is `true`, the code in the if part of the block executes. If the condition evaluates to `false`, then the code in the else part of the block executes. This can be helpful in scripts where you want a default action to happen, regardless of the conditional evaluation. For example, in our project, we always want a fortune, which is what we get in the else portion. If the fortune answers the fifth question, we want to be more selective in the response.

Manipulating the text

In this chapter, we've been capturing and storing text as a way to create a dialogue between the sprites. We use the text in a variety of ways: we type directly in a block, we access a list item, and we retrieve the text from a variable.

In programming, a piece of text is generally referred to as a string, and working with strings is a fundamental task.

Let's go beyond whole strings and look at the individual characters of a string.

Time for action – ensuring grammatically correct questions

We have a good grasp on accessing groups of words as a single item, but this exercise is going to look at the individual characters of those strings. Right now, the teller has a script that starts with the **when I receive (intro)** block. It ultimately prompts the player for a question and validates the question before issuing the answer. We're going to revise this script. The steps are as follows:

1. Detach the **broadcast (fortune)** block from the bottom of the stack and move it out of the way for now.

2. The existing **repeat until ()** block already provides a check for a minimum length and a duplicate question. We can perform a third check by adding a second **() and ()** block to the existing evaluation. You'll need to reconstruct the expression by replacing the **not ((questions) contains (answer))** expression with an **() and ()** block. The following screenshot shows the revision:

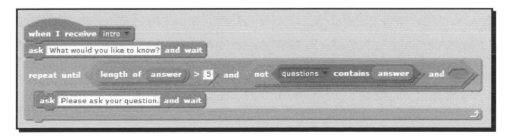

3. To the open value, we want to add the following evaluation: **((letter (length of (answer)) of (answer) = (?))**. Refer to the following screenshot for details:

4. Attach the **broadcast (fortune)** block to the end of the script.

5. If you want to revise the text in the second **ask () and wait** block, feel free to make it provide some context for the repeated question; for example, something like, `"Please ask a properly punctuated and unique question"`.

6. We now have a compact script that validates the question in three different ways.

What just happened?

With some creative block assembly, we're able to identify the last letter in our string.

When we nest blocks, Scratch evaluates the innermost block first. So, the first value evaluated in the check for the question mark is the **length of (answer)** block. This results in a number, which tells us how long the string is. That number is used as the first value of the **letter () of ()** block. The second value of the **letter () of ()** block is the answer block. Now, it's a simple equality check to see if the last letter in the answer block equals a question mark.

We structured our script such that three conditions must be true in order for the teller to provide an answer to the player. The player's question must be more than five characters long, the question must be original, and it must contain a question mark. If all three conditions are true, the teller provides an answer to the player. If any of the three conditions are false, the teller prompts the player for a new question.

Testing your project

One of my greatest joys is software testing. It's the reason I know anything about programming. The layers of question validation we're adding to the teller's script is getting more intricate as we go, which means we have lots of opportunities to create bugs. Testing our project requires deliberate steps, and it's a good idea to do some structured before you turn it loose to the greater Scratch community.

Whether you use a sheet of paper, rely on your memory, or use a spreadsheet, it helps to create a matrix of tests with the expected results. That way you can verify whether your script works as you expect it to.

The following table shows a quick matrix to help us test the question validation part of the fortune teller project:

Test	Expected result
Enter a question with three letters or characters	The teller prompts for a new question
Enter a question that's greater than five letters, is not a duplicate, and contains a question mark at the end	The teller provides a fortune to the seeker
Enter a question with more than five characters that is also a duplicate	The teller prompts for a new question
Enter an original question that is greater than five letters and does not end with a question mark	The teller reports the error and prompts for a new question
Enter a question that's greater than five letters, has a question mark, but is an exact duplicate	The teller prompts for a new question

Creating a keyword scanner

The next logical step in our project is to scan the seeker's question for individual keywords, but that will require us to write a script that analyzes the text in the answer block. We know that words are separated by spaces, so that will become the character we scan for.

Time for action – scanning a text string to build a list of words

The main task in this project is to look for spaces and create new entries in a list when we find one. Let's step through the blocks:

1. For the teller, create a new list named scanned words and a new variable named **letter#**.

2. Since we will recreate the scanned words list each time we get a new question from the seeker, we need to delete all the items before we analyze the new **answer** block value. Drag a **delete (all) from (scanned keywords)** list from the **Data** palette to the **Scripts** area.

3. Next, set the **letter#** variable to **1**, which will track our progress through the answer value.

4. To iterate through the characters in the answer value, attach a repeat **(length of (answer))** block to the stack.

5. Then, add an **if () then else** block. We will evaluate the current character of the answer value to determine if it is equal to a space. The Boolean expression will be as follows: **((letter (letter#) of (answer)) = ( ))**. You need to actually type a space in the second value of the equal to block.

6. If the condition evaluates to `true`, add an entry to the scanned words list with this **Data** block: **add () to (scanned words)**.

7. Add the **replace item (last) of (scanned words) with ()** block to the else branch of the block condition.

8. In the **with** value of the **replace item** block, add a **join** block. In value one of the **join** block, insert **item (last) of (scanned keywords)**. For value two, insert **letter (letter#) of (answer)**.

9. Finally, increment the **letter#** counter by inserting a **change (letter#) by (1)** block after the **if () then else** block.

10. Your project should already have a multiword value stored in the answers from your previous testing. Click on the stack of blocks to run the scanner. If the scanned words list monitor is not showing on the stage, then you need to show it so that you can inspect the results.

11. The good news is that the script runs and adds an entry to the scanned words list. The bad news is that the script is only adding the last word in the answer block to the list. We've got a bug.

12. The error in our script occurs in the initialization of the lists. Insert an **add () item to (scanned words)** block after the **delete (all) of (scanned words)** block. Let the value of **add** be empty. This initializes the list before we start looping through the **repeat** block. Now when you run the script, it should split the string into individual words and store all those words in the list.

13. The following screenshot shows the finished script:

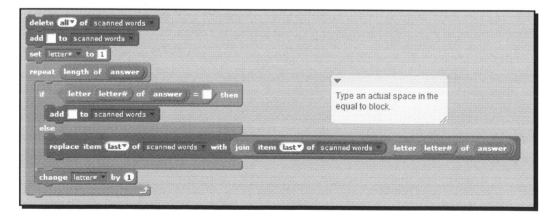

I first encountered this script on the Scratch Wiki:

`http://wiki.scratch.mit.edu/wiki/Separating_a_`
`String_Into_Wordhttp://wiki.scratch.mit.edu/wiki/`
`Separating_a_String_Into_Word`

What just happened?

We've seen most of these blocks throughout our work in this chapter. One of the keys to making the word scanner work is the iteration through each character of the answer value and tracking that progress with the **letter#** variable. I've been using letter and character interchangeably, but the script is ultimately looking for letters (for example, a, b, c), but we need to examine all the non-letter characters too. As the script examines each letter, it checks for a space. A space signals the beginning of a new word, so the **add () to ()** block adds a new empty word to the list. If you remember our previous encounter with this block, you know that the new item is added to the last position of the list.

If the player enters a question with consecutive spaces, our script will create a new item with an empty word. Depending on how you use this scanner, that may or may not be a problem.

As the script encounters a non-space letter, it joins the letter to the current item in the last position of the scanned words list, which is the partial word. This is the second key to understanding this script. For a simple example, let's assume the first word in the answer is dog. The last item in the scanned words will be "d", the first time through the loop. On pass two, the last item becomes "do". The third pass yields "dog". During the fourth pass, the script encounters a space and therefore, creates an empty word in the list. You can verify this by inserting a **say ((item (last) of (scanned words)) for (1) secs)** block after the **replace item** block.

Have a go hero – creating a more intelligent chat bot

The addition of the word scanner script opens up the possibility of scanning the answer value for a word or words that can be used to trigger a more intelligent or at least a contextual response. For example, if you scan for "chicken", you could program the teller to respond with a fortune related to chicken, such as, "Pasture raised chicken has great flavor. You will eat some in the near future".

Currently, our scanner is not integrated into any of our scripts. Your challenge is to scan the player's answer and respond based on a keyword or keywords. The teller's answer can be manually issued for each keyword, or you may create a separate list of keywords that trigger one or more alternate responses.

Oh! And don't forget to update the word scanner to ignore punctuation when scanning the answer value.

Pop quiz – understanding how to work with text

Q1. If you wanted to group ten related items together, you would create a:

1. Variable.
2. Numbers block.
3. List.
4. Forever loop.

Q2. If you want to add many items to a list at one time, how would you do it?

1. Type in each item one at a time into the add block.
2. Type in each item into the list monitor that displays on the stage.
3. Export the list from Scratch.
4. Create a list in a text file and import it via Scratch.

Q3. The mod block:

1. Modifies a number in the list.
2. Creates a variable that tracks an interval.
3. Transforms the sprite into a leprechaun.
4. Divides two numbers and reports the remainder.

Q4. We use a "counter" variable to:

1. Track how many times an event occurs.
2. Identify how many sprites we have in the project.
3. Select a random item from a list.
4. Add a new item to a specific position in the list.

Q5. Which of the following blocks gives us the exact length of a piece of text?

1. **(letter#) > (length of (answer))**
2. **Length of () from Data palette**
3. **length of () from Operators palette**
4. **item () of ()**

Summary

We're well on our way to creating an intelligent conversation with our fortune teller. I hear you. Can a conversation with a fortune teller really be intelligent? An implicit lesson in all of this is that sometimes you need a suspension of disbelief in order to enjoy a good book, a movie, or a Scratch project.

We have seen the power that the lists and variables give us to create dynamic, flexible, and fun projects. As you worked through this chapter, you probably realized that we could have used lists in some of our previous projects. For example, our scripts in *Chapter 05, Creating a Multimedia Slideshow*, would have been much smaller had we used lists. However, by avoiding lists in the earlier chapters, I ensure the projects are suitable for the youngest of Scratchers, and it sets up a nice illustration of the pragmatic usefulness of lists and variables.

By the time we finished this chapter, we have the foundation to work with a piece of text that you may encounter from list items all the way down to individual words and characters. Whether we're looping through a list, a string, or providing data validation, manipulating all that text requires a firm grasp on the use of conditional statements and control blocks.

Our programming knowledge has been accumulating nicely to this point even though you may not know it. In the next chapter, we're going to draw on everything we know as we learn to draw geometric art in Scratch. We'll turn shapes into flowers, pinwheels, and interesting patterns in addition to creating string art. We'll also explore how to use the find and use the color option in Scratch.

9
Turning Geometric Patterns into Art Using the Pen Tool

Feeling artistic? Don't worry if you're not. This is art that anyone can do. We'll make the sprite do all the hard work.

As we work our way through the chapter, we'll be programmatically creating designs in Scratch by giving the sprite a precise pattern of movements to follow. At the end of this chapter, we'll have created a shapes drawing project, a color finder application, and some string art.

These projects will have a place on their own and can be quite addictive to experiment with. However, they are highly applicable to the work we've done through the first eight chapters. These art projects, or animations, can be used in a variety of places including when the player loses in Breakout, to draw stars on a card, or as level and scene transitions.

In this chapter, we will draw on many of the concepts we've learned so far in addition to the following:

- ◆ Exploring the pen blocks to draw basic and user-defined polygons
- ◆ Capturing user input to create patterns via a custom procedure
- ◆ Understanding and using color and shade
- ◆ Drawing asymmetrical patterns and string art

Drawing basic shapes

What can you do with a triangle, square, pentagon, hexagon, octagon, and other polygons? Let's find out.

Time for action – drawing our first square

Let's start a new project and call it `shapes`. We'll work with the default cat sprite using the following steps:

1. Add the **when () key pressed** block from **Events**, and choose the letter **d** for draw. We'll use this key to draw the shape.

2. From the **Pen** palette, add the **pen down** block.

3. Attach a **move () steps** block, and set a value of 50.

4. After the **move (50) steps** block, add a **turn () degrees** block, and change the value to 90.

5. Duplicate the **move (50) steps** and **turn (90) degrees** blocks three times. Your script should look like the following screenshot:

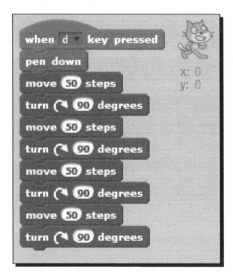

6. Press the *d* key, and observe that the cat quickly draws a square as shown in the following screenshot. Press the *d* key repeatedly, and note that the shape doesn't change.

What just happened?

We drew a square even though it happened too quickly to see, and the cat is partially obstructing the line. We'll make our script more concise soon enough, but this simple script introduces us to the **Pen** blocks in scratch. By using **pen down**, we instruct the sprite to draw using a color. Right now, we're using the default color, but we'll work on changing colors as we work through future exercises.

If you keep pressing the *d* key to redraw the square, the cat will continually retrace its path; however, its motion will be undetectable. Notice that as we move the cat, it's facing in the same direction that we started with. If we leave off the last **turn (90) degrees** block, and press the *d* key four times, the cat will draw the pattern as shown in the following screenshot:

Notice that as you draw this shape, the cat draws the smaller squares in a counterclockwise pattern. This is because after drawing the first square, the cat is facing up so that when you draw the second square, the cat first moves up before making the first 90-degree turn. And the pattern repeats until you draw one big square.

Have a go hero – exploring squares

Really quickly, explore this simple script a bit more by removing or adding the move and turn blocks in the script. For example, what pattern do you get if you remove the bottom three blocks of the script we built in the exercise?

Time for action – building on the square

Let's clean up our code, get back to a common starting position, and explore some additional shapes by performing the following steps:

1. After the **when (d) key pressed** block, add a **hide** block and a **clear** block from the **Looks** and **Pen** palettes, respectively. This will hide the sprite and remove the previous drawing if any.

2. After the **clear** block, add the **go to x: (0) y: (0)** and **point in direction (90)** blocks.

3. Now, attach a **repeat ()** block to **pen down**. Then drag the **move (50) steps** and **turn (90) degrees** blocks inside the **repeat ()** block. Delete the remaining move and turn blocks.

4. Change the value in the **repeat ()** block to 4.

5. At the end of the stack, add the **pen up** block.

6. Double-check your work by pressing the *d* key. You should get a square, and the cat should be hidden. The final script should look like the following screenshot:

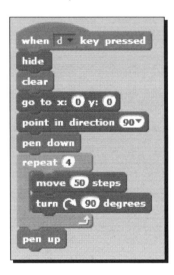

7. Now, change the value in the **repeat (4)** block to 3 and in the **turn (90) degrees** block to 120 to get a triangle.

8. Next, try repeating a 72-degree turn five times to get a pentagon.

9. Now if you repeat a 36 degree turn 10 times, you'll get a decagon.

Can you find the point at which you get a circle? As you experiment and the shape becomes too large for the stage, experiment with the length of the sides in the **move (50) steps** block.

What just happened?

Did you notice that the product of the **repeat ()** block and the **turn () degrees** block always equaled 360? By controlling the number of sides via the **repeat ()** block and the number of degrees each line moved, we were able to change shapes.

The following are the outside angles of some common shapes:

◆ A square consists of four 90 degree angles (*4 * 90 = 360*)

◆ An equilateral triangle has three 120 degree angles (*3 * 120 = 360*)

◆ A regular pentagon has five 72 degree angles (*5 * 72 = 360*)

◆ A regular octagon has eight 45 degree angles (*8 * 45 = 360*)

When we're drawing our shapes, we're calculating the exterior angles, which will total up to 360 degrees. The interior angles of various polygons will change with the shapes. For example, an equilateral triangle has three interior angles of 60 degrees each for a total of 180 degrees. The interior angles of a regular octagon are 135 degrees each.

Drawing user-defined shapes

Manually changing the values each time we want to create a different shape is a real pain, even for us, project developers. By using variables and stage **sliders**, we can very easily create a user interface that allows anyone to draw custom shapes based on the number of sides, side length, and pen size.

A user interface provides a way for people to interact with the computer program. Entire disciplines are devoted to designing user interfaces. If you think back to our joke book in *Chapter 4*, *Creating a Scratch Story Book*, the table of contents is an example of a user interface—it allowed us to select a story. The Breakout game we created in *Chapters 6*, *Making an Arcade Game – Breakout (Part 1)* uses the arrow keys as a way for the user to control the project.

Time for action – enabling the user to create custom shapes

In this exercise, we're going to create variables and enable user-entered values via sliders:

1. Create four variables named `sides`, `length`, `angle`, and `pen size`. This automatically adds a stage monitor for each variable.

2. Hide the angle stage monitor. We're going to turn the other monitors into slider controls. Right-click on each monitor and select **slider**, as shown in the following screenshot:

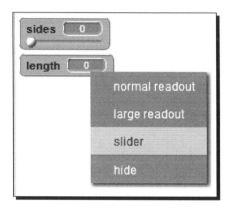

3. Next, add a **set () to** block from the **Data** palette as the first block after the **when (d) key pressed** block. We want to calculate the angle of the shape by dividing 360 by `sides`. The **set () to** block becomes **set (angle) to (360/sides)**.

4. Add the **sides** reporter block to the **repeat** block.

5. Add the **length** reporter block to the **move () steps** block.

6. Add the **angle** reporter block to the **turn () degrees** block.

7. Insert the **set pen size to ()** block above **pen down**. Add the **pen size** block as the size value in **set pen size to ()**.

8. The script looks like the following screenshot:

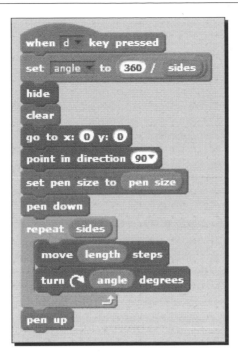

9. Now use the slider to set different values and draw. The following screenshot shows a solid octagon:

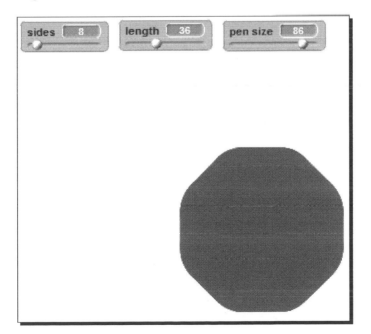

What just happened?

We've just made it incredibly easy to doodle with basic shapes. By using variables for the key values, we eliminate tedious editing of the script every time we want to create a shape. The slider control makes entering values a snap.

 Changing the stage monitor to a slider is a very popular way for Scratchers to collect user input for use in interactive games and art.

We introduced the **set pen size to ()** block, which changes the width of the line we draw. As my previous screenshot depicts, it's possible to use **set pen size to ()** to create a shape with solid colors. To create a solid square, you can set the pen size variable to the same value as the length variable. To create other shapes in a solid color, you can experiment with **pen size** and/or use a calculation of **length/tan(180/sides)** as seen in the following screenshot. The following code expressions assign the calculation to a variable named **solid pen size**, which would be used in the **set () to ()** block.

It's shown as follows for illustration purposes and won't be integrated into our project:

In the script we're building, we chose to ask the user for a number of sides, and then we used that number to calculate the angle of our shape. We could just as easily do the reverse; ask the user for the angle. Then calculate the number of sides as 360/angle. It's more likely that the user will know the number of sides.

Time for action – turning triangles into pinwheels

We're just a few blocks short of turning our basic shapes into art and patterns. Let's perform the following steps to do so:

1. Create another variable called revs (short for revolutions). We'll use this as the number of times to repeat our shape. Turn the stage monitor into a slider.

2. Enclose the **repeat (sides)** block with a new **repeat ()** block. Add the revs variable as the value in this new block.

3. Add a **turn () degrees** block after the inner **repeat (sides)** block. Use the calculation 360 divided by revs for the turn value. The final script looks like the following screenshot:

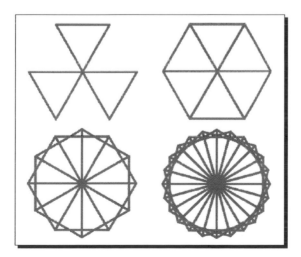

4. Now things are getting interesting. Set the values for the sides, length, revs variables as 3, 100, and 3, respectively. Then redraw the shape by changing revs to 6, 12, and 24, respectively. The following screenshot shows the pattern:

What just happened?

The `revs` variable allows the users to determine how many times to repeat the pattern, but the most important block to drawing this pattern is the **turn () degrees** block that runs after the primary shape is drawn. Without this turn block, the pattern would simply retrace its original path, and we'd only see one shape on the screen.

We calculate the number of degrees to turn by dividing 360 by the user-specified number of revolutions so that a value of 3 for `revs` will rotate 120 degrees between each pattern. This calculation ensures the pattern turns a full 360 degrees. This gets us back to the original starting point and creates symmetry. If you were to show the cat sprite, you'd see that it's still facing right at the end of this script in the middle of the stage—exactly where it started.

Have a go hero – adding a stem to the flower

Using the pen tools, draw a stem on the flower. How do you control if the stem appears in front of or behind the shape? Can you create a square flower?

Defining procedures for home and shapes

Let's take a minute to clean up our scripts and create some custom blocks for the parts of our code that we're likely to repeat from this point forward. The custom blocks will also make great additions to our Scratch Backpack.

Time for action – creating a custom shapes procedure

We're going to make procedures (custom blocks) for home and shapes. Home will initialize our drawing environment, and shapes will handle the drawing:

1. We'll start with defining a home block that sets our initial sprite position and values. From the **More Blocks** palette, click **Make a Block**, and name it `home` as a representation of an initial starting position. It will initialize the our drawing project.

2. Drag these four blocks from the existing stack, and add them to the defined home block: **hide**, **clear**, **go to x: (0) y: (0)**, and **point in direction (90)**.

3. Then use the **home** block from the **More Blocks** palette to replace the four blocks you just removed from the **when (d) key pressed** script. Check the following screenshot:

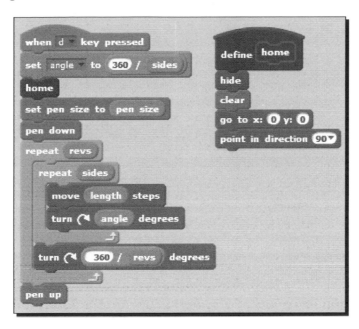

4. Next, we'll make a custom block out of the **repeat (sides)** block. Create a new custom block named **shapes** that takes three numbers as inputs: sides, length, and angle. For clarity, you should add a text label to each number input and give each input a descriptive name. You can see how I chose to do it in the next screenshot. I tried to find a balance between name length and comprehension.

5. Drag the **repeat (sides)** loop out of the existing script and attach them to the defined **shapes** block.

6. Add the **shapes** block to the script in place of the **repeat (sides)** loop we just moved. Then add the reporter blocks for **sides**, **length**, and **angle** into the respective values of the **shapes** block.

7. Go back to the **define shapes** block to do some clean up. Replace the values in the script with the custom block values. The following screenshot shows the new block and scripts:

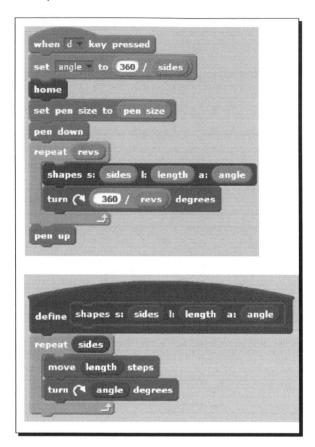

8. Take a moment to verify that your script still works.

What just happened?

After some initial experimentation, we ended up with code that will be beneficial to our other drawing projects by creating our own custom procedures. The **shapes** block now properly turns the user-specified values into the correct pattern.

Plotting the coordinates of shapes

In the examples so far, the length value controlled how long each line segment was. Even though we started at the center of the stage, we didn't need to worry about the actual coordinates of our lines. It's incredibly easy to create the patterns that we did.

Throughout the book, we've used the Cartesian coordinate system as a way to move and position sprites. The center of the stage is represented as *(0,0)*. Let's take a quick look at what it would take to draw our simple square using *x* and *y* coordinates.

Time for action – plotting x,y coordinates to draw a square

To complete this exercise, just create a new script in the existing project. That way, we can make use of our custom **home** block. Let's perform the following steps to do so:

1. Start the script with the custom **home** block, and add a **pen down** block.

2. Next, we need to add four **go to x: () y: ()** blocks. The coordinates for each block are *(100, 0)*, *(100, -100)*, *(0,-100)*, and *(0,0)* respectively.

3. Finish the stack with a **pen up** block. The following screenshot shows this quick script. As you run this stack of blocks, you'll confirm that you do, in fact, get a square.

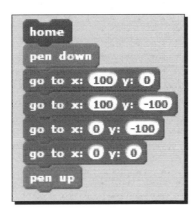

What just happened?

I picked an easy example. We're drawing the square by plotting absolute points, meaning we need to know exactly where to position the sprite in terms of its *x* and *y* positions in order to get the shape we want. Drawing a pentagon would have been much more difficult. But let's get back to the square.

In previous exercises, we rotated our shape around a center point to make a pattern. If we try to make similar patterns by plotting coordinates, we make the programming more difficult because now we'll need to know more than the number of degrees to turn. We'd need to calculate the new coordinates of the square for each revolution in the pattern, and that would simply make our life unnecessarily hard for this project.

The following screenshot represents an alternate stack of blocks that will also draw a square that is a hybrid between the move and the go to approaches:

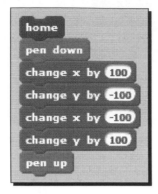

In the previous screenshot, we no longer have to worry about the coordinates of the shape. We're moving by coordinates, but it's relative to the sprite's current position. However, as the shapes get more complicated, this method will also become more difficult to use.

Can you spot the difference between the examples using the **go to x: () y: ()** and the **change by ()** blocks compared to the **move () steps** block that we built initially?

In our **shapes** procedure, we're controlling two points of movement: direction via the **turn () degrees** block and distance via the **move () steps** bock. The significance of this is demonstrated by the alternate solutions in this exercise.

Understanding and using color

Adding a splash of color can transform a cool shape into a beautiful drawing. Next, we'll look at the **set pen color to ()** and **change pen shade by ()** blocks.

Time for action – coloring our shapes

Let's take a moment to add some color to our drawing by performing the following steps:

1. In the stack that begins with **when (d) key pressed**, add a **set pen color to ()** block from the **Pen** palette below the **set pen size to (pen size)** block. Enter a value of 15.

 There are two **set pen color to ()** blocks. One is a color picker, and the other block takes a number input.

2. Now draw a shape, and you'll see that the shape is in orange color.

3. Find the **set pen shade to ()** block, and add it after the **set pen color to ()** block. Change the shade value to 25.

4. Draw the shape again while leaving the color value set to 15. The color of the shape has now changed based on the shade.

5. Let's iterate through several colors by adding a **change pen shade by ()** block inside the end of the **repeat (revs)** block. Set its value to 25.

6. Now draw the shape again, and observe the color change as each pattern gets drawn. Our script looks like the following screenshot:

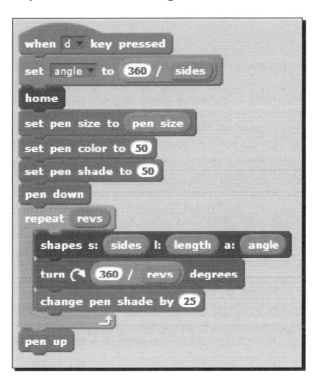

What just happened?

When we work with color, it may help us to think of color as having hue, shade, and saturation. Saturation involves the intensity of the color, but we're not going to worry about it for this discussion. Instead, we'll look at hue and shade as our previous exercise has already demonstrated. When we work with the **set pen color to ()** and **pen shade by ()** blocks, we specify a numeric value that represents the color hue.

The **set pen shade to ()** and **change pen shade by ()** blocks adjust the shade of the color, so we combine the shade and color hue as in our exercise to get different colors, such as red, orange, light blue, and dark green.

The **set pen color to ()** block takes a range from 1 to 200 before the color hues start repeating.

Our sample script shows us a very important feature of the values in Scratch's color blocks. The default shade is set to 50, which makes a color value of 15 draw in orange. Changing the shade to 25 drew a different orange.

Understanding color shades

The **set color shade to ()** block accepts a base range of 0 through 100. Shade values close to zero turn darker (for example, black) while values close to 100 turn the color lighter. However, if you enter shade values greater than 100, the dark/light color alternates. Shade values 0, 200, 400, and so on will draw dark shades. The values 100, 300, 500, and so on will draw in light shades depending on the pen color. There are still only 100 shades, but the range alternates every 100 so that 1 to 100 goes black to light, 101 to 200 goes light to black, 201 to 300 goes black to light, and so on.

Working with the set pen color to () block

The second **set pen color to ()** block is a color picker. Like the **touching color ()?** block in the **Sensing** palette, the **set pen color to ()** block with the color picker only allows you to select colors that are visible in the project editor. To use it, click on the color swatch of the block, and then click on the color you want by selecting it from anywhere in the project editor.

While this method of setting the pen color works if you want to coordinate colors with your background or sprites, or if the color you want happens to be visible in the project editor, its limited use in an art project should be self-evident. Still, picking a color like this is a lot easier than entering a random number and hoping you get a color you want.

We can create a color sprite to make picking colors easier.

Time for action – finding a color picker workaround

Let's import a color picker sprite from the book's source files so that we can have a full range of hues to select from in our art projects by performing the following steps:

1. For those of you who do not wish to or are unable to download the source files for the book, one option would be to use an image of the color picker in Scratch's paint editor. You could take a screenshot and crop the image so that only the color palette is included. Then import the new image into Scratch as a sprite.

2. The easier option is to look in the code folder for this chapter and find the image file named `Color_picker.png`.

3. From Scratch, click on the Upload sprite from the file icon. Browse for and select the `Color_picker.png` file to import it. The image file we're importing is from the Scratch Wiki; however, this is the same color picker image that can be found in the **set pen color to ()** block in Scratch 1.4.

4. Now you can select a color for use in the **set pen color to ()** block by clicking on the color swatch in the block and then clicking on the new color picker sprite.

5. The following screenshot shows the new sprite. After you pick a color, you can hide or delete the sprite to keep it out of the way of your art project.

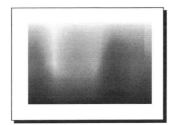

What just happened?

With a bit of creative thinking, we now have our own picker that shows the various color shades. I'd recommend adding this sprite to your backpack so that it becomes available in all your projects when you need to pick a color.

There's a change from Scratch 1.4 to 2.0 that needs to be acknowledged partially because I called it out in the exercise. In Scratch 1.4, the **set pen color to ()** and **touching ()** blocks (from **Sensing**) actually displayed a color picker similar to what we imported in the exercise, making color selection a snap. Scratch 2.0 no longer uses the color picker in conjunction with the blocks, and that was the point of the exercise.

In the **Sensing** palette, the Scratch 2.0 method makes a lot of sense as you generally only want to sense the colors of the existing costumes and backdrops. However, when you're drawing, it's safe to assume that the needed color is not visible in the project and therefore can't be selected. This exercise gave us a workaround.

Finding a color to use by its number

In the previous exercise, we imported a color picker image into Scratch that contains a wide range of hues. That's a great color selection workaround if the project creator is selecting colors and drawing. However, what if you were to create a drawing that let the user select a color value? The pickers won't work, but we could allow the users to enter number values.

It would be nice to have a reference that showed the association between numbers and colors, but there doesn't appear to be one available in the Scratch resources. So we'll create our own.

Time for action – creating a color palette

How do we know that a color value of 15 will get us orange? Let's create a simple app for that. We know that we have 200 color values, so let's script a program to draw each color value for a specified shade.

For this exercise, I'd recommend that you build the script for the color picker sprite we added in the previous exercise, and then you could add the sprite to your backpack and have both the picker and the script in one place. Let's run through this exercise, and then we'll discuss some variations. If you completed the Breakout game, then the logic for creating the color swatches in the following exercise will look familiar:

1. Since we will be repeating a pattern a set number of times, create a new variable called `count`.

2. Create a custom block named **draw colors**.

3. Let's set the starting values for our script by attaching the following blocks to the **define draw colors** block:

    ❑   **clear**

    ❑   **go to x: (-240) y: (180)**

    ❑   **set (count) to (0)**

    ❑   **set pen size to (18)**

    ❑   **set pen shade to (50)**

    ❑   **set pen color to (0)**

4. Repeat the following commands until the `count` variable is equal to `200`:

    ❑   **pen down**

    ❑   **move (35) steps**

    ❑   **pen up**

    ❑   **move (13) steps**

    ❑   **change (count) by (1)**

    ❑   **set pen color to ((count) + (1))**

5. Inside the **repeat until()** block, add an **if () then** block, and evaluate the statement **(count) mod (10) = 0**.

6. If the previous statement evaluates to true, then add **go to x: (-240) y: ((y position) – 18)** inside the **if () then** block.

7. Check your script against the following screenshot, and then run it. The following screenshot shows a two block script that can be used to clear any pen effects and then run the new **draw colors** block:

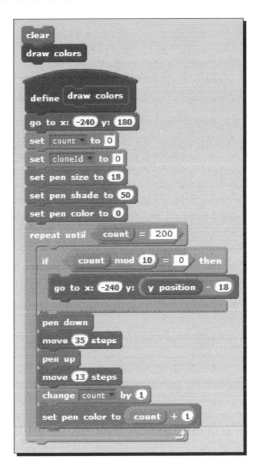

8. Adjust values in the **set pen shade to ()** block, and compare the colors you get.

The following screenshot shows the pattern of color our app creates for a shade of 50:

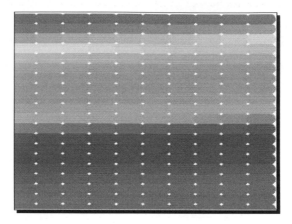

What just happened?

We just applied all of our Scratch learning to solve a problem that we encountered while trying to create another Scratch project. If you've been through all the chapters in the book so far, you'd recognize the concepts we used, including **mod** to track the pattern in order to dynamically build the rows.

We have 20 rows of 10 swatches, and numbering starts at zero in the top-left hand side corner and ends at 199 in the bottom-right hand side corner. That should allow you to find color value 15. We drew the grid of colors in such a way that you could easily pick a color and identify the corresponding number by counting. You'll have a chance to automatically report the number of each color in the next section, but before we talk about the next steps, we need to reflect on some of the math in the current exercise.

The pattern shown in the previous screenshot will take up the entire stage, which is why we started at *(-240, 180)*. We're drawing 10 colors per row for a total of 20 rows. That gives us 200 colors. In order to make each row span the width of the stage, we need to make each color take up 48 pixels. Our script actually uses two **move () steps** blocks to get this done. We first set the **move (35) steps** block, put the **pen up** block, and then set the **move (13) steps** block. This creates the visual whitespace you'll see in the pattern of colors. If you use a **single move (48) steps** block, there would be no visual separation. We use 48 in our calculations because the stage is 480 pixels wide, and when we divide 480 by 10, we get 48.

To move the pattern down the stage horizontally, we need to know that the stage is 360 pixels tall, so when we divide 360 by 20 we get 18. We make 18 the pen size, and we move the rows down the stage by 18 pixels.

I'd suggest adding this script to your backpack as well.

Have a go hero – finding all shades for a color

There are multiple ways to build upon the color app we just created. We have a quick way to see all the color hues for a specified shade. The following are a few potential modifications:

◆ The script can be duplicated and modified to draw the shades of a specified color.

◆ You can also create a script that reports the color number when you click on a point on the stage. The code sample includes a possible solution by first determining the *x* position and then the *y* position. If you think carefully about the numbers that we used and talked about, you'll have a good starting point. I'll give you a hint by giving you the coordinate to identify the position on the *x* axis. The missing part of the script in the following screenshot is calculating the row based on the *y* coordinate.

◆ You can develop an application that draws all 100 shades for each of the 200 color hues. If you want inspiration for that, check out the project at `http://scratch.mit.edu/projects/18089786/`. Actually, this project will give you some hints about how to use the mouse cursor to identify a point on the color picker that we built. However, it won't translate directly to the version that we created in our exercise, but it does get you in the right direction.

Adding color slider inputs to the shapes project

As one of the last pieces of customization to this project, let's give the user a way to add color via a stage slider just as we do for `sides`, `length`, `pen size`, and `revs`.

Time for action – limiting color values with a slider

Let's perform the following steps to limit color values via the slider:

1. We have two color values to manipulate, so create two more variables with the names `color` and `shade`. Turn each new variable into a slider control on the stage.

2. Let's limit the input that the user can enter. Right-click on the color slider, and select the option **set slider min and max**. This will open a **Slider Range** dialog box as shown in the following screenshot:

3. In the **Min** and **Max** fields, enter 0 and 199 respectively. Click on **OK** to save the range.
4. Test the slider control out, and verify that you cannot select a value higher than 199.
5. Now incorporate the color and shade variables into the appropriate blocks in the script as shown in the following screenshot:

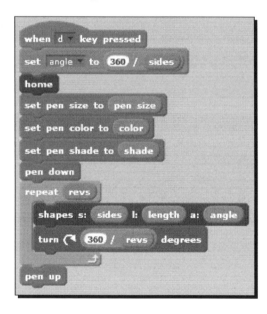

What just happened?

Now, every value in our shapes project can be set by the user via slider controls that are displayed on the stage. This exercise showed us that we can force the user to enter a range of values via the **set slider min and max** option, which is obviously very useful when we want to restrict values that a user can enter via the slider controls. In a Scratch project, a non-programming user will have access to edit the project, but we assume that most of our users will interact with the project via the user interface we designed. And you'll notice that if you try to move the slider all the way to the edges, it never passes the defined range.

Even with the sliders, as programmers, we can still use the **set () to ()** block to assign any value we want to the variable. The slider controls only limits the the values through the user interface.

Have a go hero – expanding the shapes application

The shapes application we created has a lot of potential, and it seems to be well suited to exploring symmetrical patterns of different shapes. The interface could use some refinements before being published to the Scratch community. One recommendation would be to hide the sliders when the user draws the shape. That way you can use the entire screen to draw. That would require an extra step to reset the sliders on the stage perhaps when the green flag is clicked. You also need to provide some instructions to the user.

Technically, what else can you do with this basic shape drawing application? Can you move the pattern to a different spot on the stage and draw multiple copies? Maybe you can ask the user for the number of times to repeat the entire pattern and then write the script to arrange that pattern on the stage using all the user-defined information. Still, another idea would be to instruct the user to click on a point on the stage and then draw the pattern around that point.

Creating asymmetrical patterns

While our work in this chapter has been interesting and insightful, everything has been symmetrical. In the next exercise, we're going to create a new explosion pattern with ever increasing line lengths and odd angles.

Time for action – creating an explosion

Let's draw a pattern, and then we'll completely change the pattern by changing a couple of key values. You don't have to, but I'm going to start with a new project.

1. Create a variable named `counter`. Let's initialize our script with the following set of blocks:

   ❑ **clear**

   ❑ **go to x: (0) y: (0)**

   ❑ **set (counter) to (1)**

   ❑ **pen down**

2. Add a **repeat ()** block and change the value to `125`.

3. Repeat the following set of blocks:

   ❑ **move ((counter) * (2)) steps**

   ❑ **turn (204) degrees**

   ❑ **change (counter) by (1)**

4. Next, finish the script by adding the **pen up** block outside the loop.

5. Check your script against the following screenshot, and then draw the shape:

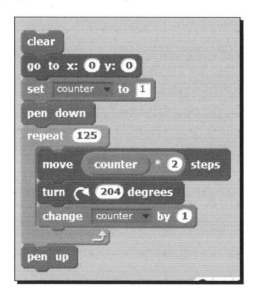

6. First, remove the **(counter) * (2)** block from the **move () steps** block. Then change the value in the **move () steps** block to `100`, and draw the shape.

7. Now put the **(counter) * (2)** block back into in the **move () steps** block. Then change the value in the **turn ()** block to 185, and draw the shape.

8. The following screenshot shows the three patterns we just drew. Can you figure out how to draw the fourth pattern?

9. You might notice that some of the patterns have a tag end visible where the pattern stops. You can clean that up by adding a **move (60) steps** block after the **repeat ()** loop. That will not work with the symmetrical pattern that we drew using the **move (100) steps** version. Experimentation is the name of the game.

What just happened?

We created a simple but cool project. Our first twist is the use of the counter variable. In the past, we've used this type of variable to control the number of times to loop through the **repeat()** block. Even though counter tracks the number of times the pattern has run, it's used as a multiplier in the **move () steps** block.

We demonstrated the impact the **(counter) * (2)** calculation had on the **move () steps** block by removing it and using a constant number, such as 100. The pattern became very even compared with the explosive appearance of the original calculation.

 If you want an easy way to slow down and see the pattern develop, add a **wait (.3) secs** block at the end of the **repeat ()** loop.

Turning straight lines into string art

So far, we've used the pen tools to draw patterns using angles and forward movements to trace a continuous path. For our next art project, let's straighten our movements out and create something using nothing but straight lines, which is a technique often called string art. The lines will not be continuous.

Time for action – animating a radar screen

To pull off a radar pattern, we'll rotate straight lines around a circle, but we'll need to draw upon our earlier work with colors to make the animated effect. Let's create a new stack of blocks by performing the following steps:

1. Let's initialize our starting point with the following blocks:
    - **clear**
    - **go to x: () y: ()**
    - **set pen shade to (50)**
    - **pen down**

2. Then add a **forever** block. We want to repeat the following set of blocks:
    - **set pen size to (1)**
    - **turn (90) degrees**
    - **set pen color to (15)**
    - **move (60) steps**
    - **move (60) steps**
    - **set pen size to (1)**
    - **set pen color to (101)**
    - **move (-120) steps**
    - **turn (1) degrees**

3. When you run the script, you should get a pattern similar to the following screenshot. As the pattern repeats, the thin, dark lines create a movement around the center point while the background color remains solid. It's a relatively noisy pattern.

To speed up the pattern, use the turbo mode by shift-clicking the green flag.

4. Now let's experiment a bit. To see the effect properly, rerun the script so that the previous pattern clears. Set the first **set pen size to ()** block value to 20, and note the change in the animation.

5. Now change the value in the second **set pen size to ()** block to 10.

6. For the next animation, change the value in the third **move () steps** block to -60, and update the last **turn () degrees** block to 5 degrees.

7. The following screenshot shows a snapshot each of the animations we just created:

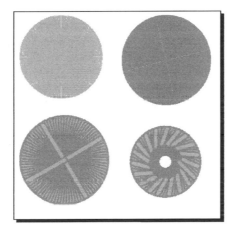

What just happened?

To create these animations, we're not only drawing on our recently discovered color knowledge, but we're moving forward and then retracing the line to create some curious effects. It's the combination of color and movement that creates the visible animation in the pattern.

Remember what we said about color? The smaller numbers such as 15 will be darker, while the larger number such as 101 will be lighter. The first two **move () steps** blocks move forward 60 steps each in the orange color. The third **move () steps** block advances -120 steps, retracing the original forward movement; however, this time the color is a light blue, which becomes the dominant color.

There's a lot happening in the animation. There is a **turn (90) degrees** block at the beginning of the loop, and at the end we have a **turn (1) degrees** block. This second turn will ensure that the pattern eventually overlaps itself. If we run this animation at normal speed and not in turbo mode, we notice that it takes many revolutions before we see the noisy pattern of the darker line shows up. Running in turbo mode enhances the visual effect. The combination of the speed of the animation combined with the slight hesitation caused by the two consecutive **move (60) steps** blocks appears to be the primary reason we see the pattern, because if we consolidate the two **move (60) steps** blocks with a single **move (120) steps** block, the pattern disappears.

In our fourth pattern, we shortened the backward movement to half of what the forward movement was; the thick orange circle in the middle of the pattern is a direct result of that uneven movement. The bigger angle at the end of the pattern creates a thicker blue line.

Time for action – breaking out of the circle

Not all of our art needs to create a circle, and just to prove it, the following is a quick example:

1. For this pattern, we'll use a variable called `counter` as both a way to control the number of times to repeat the pattern and a multiplier for the ever-changing *x* and *y* coordinates. Create the variable, if you don't have one in your current project.

2. Set the initial values for the pattern as shown in the following set of blocks:
   - **set (counter) to (0)**
   - **clear**
   - **hide**
   - **set pen size to (1)**

3. Add a **repeat () until** block and use the condition **(counter) > (25)** as the value. Repeat the following set of blocks:
   - **pen up**
   - **go to x: ((counter) * (10) y: (0)**
   - **pen down**
   - **go to x: (0) y: (250) – ((counter) * (10))**
   - **change (counter) by (1)**

4. The resulting pattern should match the following screenshot:

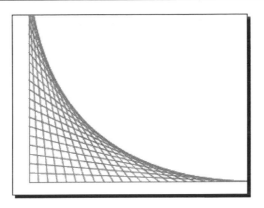

What just happened?

The key to this pattern is the use of the `counter` variable as a multiplier. The pattern starts at *(0, 0)* and moves right along the *x* axis in increments of 10 with each iteration, which is controlled by the calculated value of **counter * 10**.

The second **go to x: () y: ()** block calculates the destination point of the line, which is constantly dropping vertically. If we were to slow this pattern down with a **wait ()** block, we'd be able to see that at about the sixth pass, the line crosses the top of the pattern for the first time, creating the curved perspective—all without a **turn () degrees** block, you'll note.

There's another significant value in this script. The loop is repeating 25 times and we're using a calculation of **250 – (counter) * (10)** to draw. Repeating 20 times would not give us the same complete pattern, while 30 would be too much. If we repeat the pattern 30 times, we would need to calculate the *y* coordinate as **300 – (counter) * (10)**. See a pattern?

Have a go hero – twisting your perspective

Can you twist your perspective to figure out how to draw the following pattern?

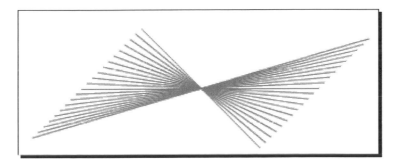

Pop quiz – getting into shape

Q1. If you want to draw a square and an octagon, what is the sum of the all the exterior angles in the shape?

1. You can't do that.
2. 90 degrees.
3. 45 degrees.
4. 360 degrees.

Q2. If you want to select a light shade, which of the following shade values would you use in the **set pen shade to ()** block?

1. 0.
2. 10.
3. 100.
4. 200.

Q3. How can you restrict the user input to a variable with a slider stage monitor?

1. Users should never be able to control a variable.
2. The slider control cannot be restricted.
3. Right-click on slider, and use the **set slider min and max** option.
4. Write a script to validate the user entry.

Summary

Whether it's the simple elegance of a square rotating 18 times in 20 degree increments or animated string art, there is a lot to be fascinated by in this chapter. What's more, you could spend hours exploring these patterns one angle at a time. While not every project has a need for drawings, adding a strategic drawing to help with level transitions or as an indicator that something happened can add a nice design touch.

The color sprite and app we created in this chapter should go into your backpack so that they are available for use in all your Scratch projects. You never know when you need to find a specific color. Likewise, the custom blocks we created for our home and shapes projects would be nice additions to your backpack.

In the next chapter, we'll explore our physical world by adding the PicoBoard, our webcam, and our computers' built-in microphone to our Scratch projects. We'll capture environmental effects that we can use to control our projects or that we can display via a Scratch-generated graph.

Connecting a PicoBoard to Scratch 1.4

There are various ways to connect Scratch to the physical world, including Makey Makey, LEGO® WeDo, Raspberry Pi, and PicoBoard. Even though all of these devices require add-on hardware to interact with Scratch, they extend the Scratch experience and enable Scratch projects to connect to the physical world.

We're going to use the PicoBoard as the basis for our examples, because it tends to be one of the most popular devices used with Scratch and has a long history with the Scratch team. With slight modifications, each project can be adapted to work without a PicoBoard, and therefore, to work with Scratch 2.0.

In this appendix, I will introduce the PicoBoard and show you how to:

◆ Animate webcam images based on detected sound

◆ Monitor and collect environmental data and then graph the results

◆ Explore electrical resistance

As of the publication of this book update, Scratch 2.0 does not have full support for add-on hardware such as the PicoBoard; however, the Scratch team foresees full support at some point in 2014. Until Scratch 2.0 fully supports the PicoBoard, you may use Scratch 1.4 to complete these projects.

I've selected projects that have components that will apply to Scratch 2.0 right now, including the webcam, detecting sound, recording data at set intervals, and graphing. The fact that I choose to use the PicoBoard to develop these projects acknowledges the wealth of opportunity to extend Scratch. It's also a nod to Raspberry Pi users for whom Scratch 2.0 is not currently an option, but the PicoBoard works on the Pi.

Using Scratch 1.4, the PicoBoard, and Raspberry Pi

Until Scratch 2.0 fully supports the PicoBoard, you'll need to use Scratch 1.4 to interact with the PicoBoard. It just so happens that the Raspberry Pi only supports Scratch 1.4 at this time, and the PicoBoard will work just fine on the Pi. Pi users are a custom-built audience for Scratch and hardware such as the PicoBoard.

If you run a Linux-based system, then your choice of Scratch versions gets more complicated. Adobe, the developer of Flash, has announced that it's no longer supporting AIR or Flash on Linux after Version 11.2 of its player unless you're running the Chrome browser. Adobe and Google have a deal to provide a Chrome-only plugin. If you work in an open source operating system world, then you know the intricacies and frustrations of managing mainstream software from companies such as Adobe.

We won't get sidetracked here. Just know that if you're on an open source operating system and you have problems with Scratch 2.0, then seek out the 1.4 Version. You'll still have a great experience.

 The bottom line is that it appears as if Scratch 1.4 will coexist with Scratch 2.0 for the foreseeable future. Your chances of encountering 1.4 are great.

Finding Scratch 1.4

Scratch 1.4 is available from the following resources:

◆ Installable version: `http://scratch.mit.edu/scratch_1.4/`

◆ Source code: `http://info.scratch.mit.edu/Source_Code`

Purchasing the PicoBoard

The PicoBoard is an add-on piece of hardware that has sensors to detect the amount of light, sound, and resistance. There is also a slider controller and a button. Today, the PicoBoard is manufactured and sold by SparkFun (`https://www.sparkfun.com/products/10311`), but previous versions of the board were sold by PicoCricket. Consult the manufacturer for installation instructions.

Time for action – enabling and testing the PicoBoard support in Scratch 1.4

The blocks we need to interact with the PicoBoard are hidden by default. Let's enable them by proceeding with the following steps:

1. Plug your PicoBoard in to your computer and start Scratch. In the **Sensing** palette, there are two blocks related to the PicoBoard: the **() sensor value** reporter block and the **sensor ()** Boolean block as shown in the following screenshot:

2. Let's ensure we have a signal. Click on the checkbox for the **(slider) sensor value** block to show the stage monitor.

3. Then move the slider back and forth and ensure that a value is being reported as you move the slider. The following screenshot shows the stage monitor:

4. If the block is not detecting a value, double-check your connections, and ensure you have the drivers from the manufacturer installed correctly. You should also close Scratch and reopen it.

What just happened?

The PicoBoard is connected, and Scratch is reading values from the board. The **() sensor value** and **sensor ()** blocks will be used as values and conditional evaluations for many other blocks in Scratch.

Adding the PicoBoard support to Scratch 2.0

I know what you're thinking. At the beginning of this appendix, I said Scratch 2.0 doesn't support the PicoBoard—at publication, that's true. You can check if PicoBoard is supported in 2.0 by shift-clicking on the **More Blocks** palette. That will display an **Add an Extension** button, which will give you access to **Extension Library**.

If PicoBoard is available, it will be an option in **Extension Library**. You can select it, and then test the PicoBoard just as we did in the previous exercise. At various times, the PicoBoard option has appeared and reappeared in **Extension Library**, but it's only a guess as to when the support might officially show up in Scratch 2.0.

The following screenshot shows the proposed PicoBoard blocks in 2.0 (from a time when the extension was available):

You can keep yourself updated on Scratch 2.0 and the PicoBoard support via the following resources:

◆ Scratch News: `http://scratch.mit.edu/news`

◆ How to connect to Physical World: `http://wiki.scratch.mit.edu/wiki/How_to_Connect_to_the_Physical_World` and `http://scratch.mit.edu/newshttp://wiki.scratch.mit.edu/wiki/How_to_Connect_to_the_Physical_World`

◆ Connecting to the Physical World forum: `http://scratch.mit.edu/discuss/32/`

Animating webcam images by detecting sound

One of the coolest features of Scratch is its ability to work with your computer's webcam. The ability to incorporate backdrops (in Scratch 2.0), backgrounds in Scratch 1.4, and sprites by taking pictures with the webcam has been a long-time feature of Scratch, including the current version. In this project, we'll incorporate webcam photos with a sound sensor on the PicoBoard.

Don't have a PicoBoard? Then I'll show you how to use the computer's built-in microphone.

Time for action – creating a talking head

In previous examples, we've seen how easy it is to import images from Scratch's built-in libraries or from files on our computer. Now, it's time to circle back and check out the webcam. This exercise will also use the PicoBoard's sound sensor to detect our voice.

To start, create a new project, and delete or hide the Scratch cat and then complete the following steps:

1. With the stage selected, click on the **Backgrounds (Backdrops In 2.0)** tab, and then click on the camera icon. A new window is displayed and shows what the webcam sees.

On Scratch 2.0, an Adobe Flash Player settings' dialog box will prompt you to allow or deny access to the computer's camera and microphone. You must allow access in order to use the webcam.

2. Look at the camera with your mouth closed, and click on the camera icon to import the image. Then open your mouth, and take another snapshot. Click on **Done** to close the dialog box. We now have two background images.

3. Name the first imported image `silent` and the second one `talking`.

4. Now let's script our snapshots. Click back to the **Scripts** tab, and start with a **when flag clicked** block.

5. Add a **switch to background ()** block, and select the silent background. This block is called **switch backdrop to ()**.

6. Now we'll need to continually evaluate whether or not the detected sound sensor value is greater than 15.

7. Add a **forever** block followed by an **if (), else** block from the **Controls** palette. Add the greater-than block to the condition value. From the **Sensing** palette, add the **() sensor value** block, and select the **sound** sensor. Enter `15` for the block's second value.

 If you are completing this exercise without the PicoBoard, substitute the **loudness** block for **() sensor value** to use the computer's built-in microphone.

8. If the sound is greater than 15, we want to alternate between the two backgrounds. Add a **switch background to (talking)** block, followed by a **wait (.1) secs** block, which is then followed by a **switch background to (silent)** block.

9. As the else condition, add a **switch backdrop to (silent)** block.

10. Click on the green flag and talk. Feel free to experiment with the detected loudness value and the wait value of the script to see what effects you end up with.

11. Let's make one more enhancement to this script to give our animation the feel of a 1980s television station that went off air. Add the following block to the if condition: **set (ghost) effect to ((100) – ((sound) sensor value)**. Then to the else condition, add this block: **set (ghost) effect to (100)**. Depending on how loudly you talk, you might want to experiment with multiplying the (sound) sensor value by some number, such as five. Now the image will fade in and out based on the loudness. The following screenshot shows our script:

```
when   clicked
forever
    if        sound   sensor value  >  15
        set  ghost   effect to  100 -   sound   sensor value
        switch to background  talking
        wait  0.1  secs
        switch to background  silent
    else
        set  ghost   effect to  100
        switch to background  silent
```

What just happened?

By combining the backgrounds that we saved from the computer's webcam and the detected sound levels, we very quickly and easily integrated external data into our Scratch project. The fact that our talking head looks a little goofy makes it fun. It reminds me of translated movies where the English translation is dubbed in over the original movie. The sound never quite matches the mouth movements, but it is often close enough to get the point across.

By adjusting the ghosting effect, we took some of the emphasis off the timing of the script. The visual strength of the image depends on the strength (loudness) of the detected sound. With the sound sensor on the PicoBoard, a higher sound value corresponds to a louder noise. The sensor will report values from 0 to 100 like the loudness block.

When we apply the ghosting affect while speaking, we calculate the new ghost value by subtracting the sound value from 100. You'll need to experiment with your sounds, but if the sensor measures a sound value of 20, then the ghost value becomes 80. This ensures our image is visible but not in full strength. Remember that with ghost, 0 is fully visible and 100 is transparent.

Have a go hero – using sound to move a sprite forward and backward

The talking head makes a great way to introduce Scratch programming in the physical world because it's quirky and generally makes people chuckle. It's really well suited for an audience such as workshops or presentations. I've seen this project done with animated lips, and I've used it in the past to strobe two colors based on the sound.

You could also use the sound value in other projects to change a sprite's costume, to move a sprite, or to apply a graphical effect. Explore the sound values some more by writing a script that moves a sprite forward and backward based on the detected loudness of the sound.

Sharing Scratch 1.4 projects online

If you create a project in Scratch 1.4, you can still share that project to the new Scratch 2.0 website. Other people will be able to view your project on the website. The Scratch 2.0 website will not export a 1.4 file, and as soon as you edit the older file online, it will be saved as a new Scratch 2.0 format.

 You can tell a Scratch 1.4 file by its file extension; they end in .sb while Scratch 2.0 projects have a .sb2 extension.

Sensing the environment with the PicoBoard

Each of the PicoBoard's sensors is described in the following table:

Sensor	Values	Description
sound	0 to 100	Captures the sound from via the board's built-in microphone. A quiet noise will register a lower value than a louder noise.
light	0 to 100	A higher value means that the sensor is detecting more light. As you block light from reaching the sensor, it reports lower values.
button	true or false	Clicking on the button causes the sensor to register a true value, and it will continue to register a true value for as long as the button is pressed.
slider	0 to 100	Move the slider to select a value. Could be used to provide numeric input, such as setting the size of a sprite to the selected value.
resistance	0 to 100	The board includes four analog ports (A, B, C, D) with alligator clips to measure the resistance in a circuit.

Measuring resistance

The PicoBoard comes with four analog ports labelled A through D. Each port has its own set of alligator clips to form circuits. We'll be connecting a **thermistor** to the alligator clips in order to record the **resistance** of the thermistor over time. We'll complete this project in two exercises: one to record values and the other to chart the values.

Thermistors are commonly used as temperature sensors, and the next exercise will show us how to collect values from our thermistor that can be used in conjunction with temperature-based experiments. Wikipedia states that:

> *A thermistor is a type of resistor whose resistance varies significantly with temperature, more so than in standard resistors.*

Thermistors are inexpensive and available from electric supply outlets that can be found online and in stores near you.

Time for action – recording the resistance of a thermistor over time

The following exercise walks us through creating a script that records resistance values based on an interval. If you don't have a PicoBoard or a thermistor, you could alter the script to record loudness. We're going to be setting up this project as a way to conduct experiments with resistance, and because we're using the thermistor, we can draw some conclusions about temperature.

We'll create the framework to do the monitoring, and at the end of this exercise, you'll have a thermistor measuring the resistance at room temperature. (Non-PicoBoard users can set this framework up with the **loudness** block to capture sound.)

We'll discuss ways to apply our environmental monitor in other interesting ways after we get the framework finished up. We create the framework as follows:

1. Let's set up our project. Create a new project, and replace the Scratch cat with a small circle sprite that you create in the paint editor. You may name it circle sprite.

2. Add a new list called **measurements** as a place to store the collected results.

3. Make sure the PicoBoard is connected to the computer and has one of the alligator clips plugged into one of the ports.

4. Connect one lead of the alligator clip to one lead of the thermistor. Attach the second clip to the other lead of the thermistor.

5. Next, add the **when flag clicked** block to the **Scripts** area. Attach the following blocks to initialize the project:

   - **hide**
   - **delete (all) of (measurements)**
   - **add (resistance-B) sensor value to (measurements)**

6. Add a **forever** block to the script so we can continually run the following blocks:

   □ **wait (60 secs)**

   □ **add (resistance-B) sensor value to (measurements)**

7. The following screenshot shows the script. Note that this script will run forever. We'll review why I chose this script in the upcoming discussion.

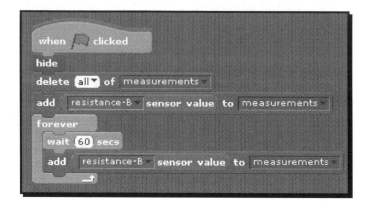

What just happened?

If we examine the values that we recorded in the measurements list, they likely do not vary significantly at room temperature. The key control point of this script is the interval at which we collect information. Basically, we collect a sample every 60 seconds. We actually record a measurement before we start the forever loop, which gives us a reading at minute zero that which would correspond to the start of the experiment, assuming we use this script as the basis for the experiment.

The script, as written, is an infinite loop. I'm okay with that. The real question is, are you? The reason I chose not to provide an exit for the data collection is that it may be difficult to know how long the script should run, and depending on what you choose to measure, you will be present to manually stop the script and the collection. If you measure the resistance of boiling water, you'd be present. If you measure the warming of water from solid ice to room temperature, you're not sure how long that would take. So, you could set the script and come back several hours later to check on it.

In other words, you pressing the stop button in the project is the condition that stops the data collection. For example, if you wanted to ensure that you had an exact number of measurements, you could replace the **forever** block with a **repeat ()** block. Your choice!

The data we collect is dependent on using the alligator clips to form a circuit using the thermistor. As I alluded, thermistors can be used to calculate a temperature based on the measured resistance. A widely used formula called the Steinhart-Hart equation (`http://en.wikipedia.org/wiki/Steinhart%E2%80%93Hart_equation`) can be used to calculate a temperature in Kelvin based on resistance values that could then be converted to Fahrenheit or Celcius.

Scratch interprets resistance on a scale from 0 to 100, which limits our ability to perform the actual temperature calculation based on the measured resistance. For now, the recorded resistance values could be used to make observations about temperature; the actual temperature calculation is not a goal of our exercises.

Completing a circuit

When we connect the alligator clips together, we basically replicate a switch, like the one that turns the light in the room on and off. Connect the clips to complete the circuit (that is, turn it on). Remove one clip to break the circuit (that is, turn it off). In Scratch, a resistance value of 100 is equivalent to off; no current passes through the circuit. A resistance value of 0 means that current is flowing freeing through the circuit without any resistance. Values between 0 and 100 measure the amount in the circuit.

The following screenshot illustrates the resistance values. The value in **resistance-A** is **100.0** because the alligator clips are not connected. The **53.8** value for **resistance-B** is the resistance value recorded by a thermistor at room temperature (approximately 70 degrees Fahrenheit), and the **resistance-C** value of **0.0** is a circuit with no resistance from two alligator clips connected together.

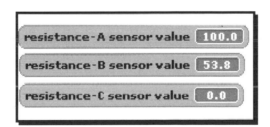

The **loudness** reporter block is working in a similar way. A loudness value of 0 means there is no detected sound, while a value of 100 indicates maximum loudness (as measured by Scratch).

You can only create a circuit using the alligator clips attached to a single sensor. In other words, connecting the clips on sensor A to sensor B will not create a circuit and the values for sensors A and B will remain 100.

When we measure electrical resistance, we want to know by how much the material impedes an electrical current. In the case of our PicoBoard sensor, the higher the value, the more the material impedes the current. How we use that value is left to our imagination and the needs of our project.

Time for action – charting our measurements

Now that we have some data in our measurements list, we can create a graph to display the results. If you did not collect a list of measurements through the previous exercise, you can import `0724OS_measurements.txt` from the book's code files into your measurements list. If you remember our work with lists in *Chapter 8, Chatting with a Fortune Teller*, you recall that you can import a list by showing the list monitor, right-clicking on the monitor, and choosing import. Then you'll have everything you need in order to create a graph. The following screenshot shows what our finished graph will look like:

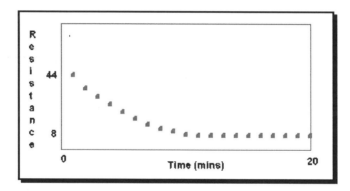

I haven't told you much about a thermistor's relationship with temperature and resistance yet, which makes drawing any conclusions about the graph difficult. We'll get there, but first, let's chart the data as follows:

1. Create a new variable named `count` that we can use as a way to track our script's position in the **measurements** list.

2. We'll use the **when (g) key pressed** block as the event to draw the graph. Our first group of blocks will initialize our drawing conditions as follows:

    ❑ **point in direction (90)**

    ❑ **clear**

    ❑ **set size to (5) %** (You may need to adjust this percentage based on the original size of your circle sprite.)

❏ **set (count) to (1)**

❏ **pen up**

❏ **go to x: (-150) y: (0)**

❏ **pen down**

3. We should recognize the border around the graph as a rectangle. To draw the rectangle, repeat the following blocks two times:

❏ **move 300 steps**

❏ **turn clockwise 90 degrees**

❏ **move 150 steps**

❏ **turn 90 degrees**

❏ **pen up**

4. Stop drawing by adding the **pen up block after the repeat (2)** block.

5. Now we plot the points. To ensure we see the circle sprite, add a **show** block. Add a **repeat ()** block with the following value, which will represent the number of times to repeat the blocks: **(length of (measurements)**. Then repeat the following blocks:

❏ **go to x: () y: ()**

❏ **stamp**

❏ **change (count) by (1)**

6. Let's fill in the **x:** value of the **go to** block with a simple calculation **(x position) + (15)**. Based on our recorded data, this makes one minute equal to 15 pixels, which runs along the *x* axis.

7. For the **y:** value, we'll use **(item (count) of (measurements)) * (2)**. This means that we scale each resistance value to two pixels so that a resistance value of 44 will be plotted at 88 on the *y* axis. This spreads our data out to present a more readable format.

8. After the **repeat (length of (measurements)** block, add a **hide** block so that the circle sprite is no longer visible. Our finished script looks like the following screenshot:

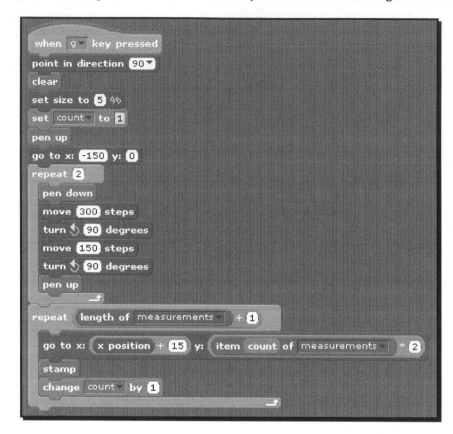

9. You can finish up the graph by adding some labels as seen in the screenshot at the top of the exercise. Using the paint editor to create labels that you position on the stage to represent key points would be sufficient.

What just happened?

We've used all of the previous concepts throughout the book. The key to making our graph display is determining how to scale our graph to fit onto the Scratch stage. I made a decision to run the *x* axis in the center of the screen at *y*=0.

Our test data was a small sample size, so we actually scaled up to make the graph legible; if you end up with a lot of data that exceeds your screen size, you would have to scale the graph down. Making each minute correspond to five pixels instead of 15 pixels could be an example.

To scale the resistance value on the *y* axis, we scaled those values up. Knowing some basic information about what we're graphing certainly helps make these decisions. For example, examining the measurements, I knew the largest value was 44, and we drew the chart boundary to be 150 pixels tall. Scaling the resistance values by two means that my first point is plotted 88 pixels high on the graph's *y* axis, and everything looks just fine.

We also use the **stamp** tool from the **Pen** palette to place individual dots, but a bigger dataset might be better served by drawing the curve with a continuous line.

Interpreting the graph

I've been holding back some information about a thermistor, but that information is important to understanding what we're graphing. As the temperature rises, the resistance of the thermistor decreases. So, that means our graph (in the 07240S_measurements.txt list) is charting a rising temperature. That graph is shown as follows:

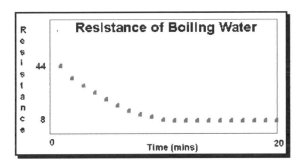

As you see from the graph's now-visible title, the graph is charting the change in temperature by way of the resistance as the water rises to boil. Because this is the type of experiment where you would be monitoring things very closely, you'd know through observation that the water started to boil at approximately 12 minutes, which is represented by the levelling out of the points on the graph. Looking at the actual values in the **measurements** list, we see that the resistance levels out at 8.2, making 8.2 the resistance of boiling water as observed with this thermistor.

This project is more about showing you the possibilities of using a PicoBoard to conduct experiments and less about teaching you that the temperature of water does not rise the longer it boils.

The graph labels are highlighting key values. The 44 on the resistance (*y* axis) is marking the first recorded value. On the *x* axis, we measure time, starting at 0 and ending at 20 minutes.

The first point on the graph is representing our first resistance value of 44 (44.1 actually). As the water warmed, the resistance dropped until the twelfth minute. At minute 12, the water was in a rolling boil, which is 212 degrees Fahrenheit. From that point on, the resistance was flat, meaning the water doesn't get hotter the longer it boils.

If this was a temperature graph, we would expect to see the graph rise as the temperature approached boiling. However, with a thermistor, as the temperature rises, the resistance falls. The graph is accurately describing what happens with the resistance as the water heats.

And here's a general disclaimer. I collected my measurements by suspending the thermistor into the top one-fourth inch of water and protecting my PicoBoard from the heat source. I'm not responsible for your actions. Only do experiments if you think through your safety and consequences. Suspending a thermistor in ice water and measuring values as the water warms to room temperature would be a less risky alternative.

Time for action – revising the graph

As you see in the previous screenshot, the first point on the graph is moved to the right by 15 pixels. Our first measurement in the data that we graphed occurred at zero minutes is not accurately reflected in our graph. Let's make the graph match the numbers more closely by moving the circle sprite to the left for the first point as follows:

1. Add a **go to x: () y: ()** block before the **repeat ()** block.
2. Add the expression **((x position) – (15))** to the **x** value.
3. Add the expression **((item (count) of (measurements) * (2))** to the **y** value. The following screenshot shows the revised script:

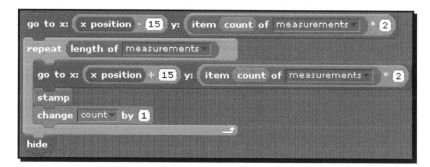

What just happened?

Our initial graph didn't properly mark the first point at zero minutes. In our revised script, we moved the circle sprite to the left by 15 pixels so that when we graph the first point in the **repeat (length of (measurements))** block, the point was placed properly on the graph.

Have a go hero – brainstorming data collection topics

Unless you're monitoring a doorway that frequently opens and closes, recording the room temperature probably doesn't provide much excitement. Other items to measure might include a pot of boiling water or measuring how long it takes for a glass of ice water to reach room temperature.

You could also run a series of resistance tests with common materials. For example, attach the alligator clips to a potato, a paper clip, and so on. Record the values and then graph the results. You may need to modify the collection framework to record a value based on the occurrence of an event such as the button click on the PicoBoard or a key press on the keyboard.

Let's see what you can come up with!

Pop quiz – connecting to the real world

Q1. What Scratch block can provide an alternative to the PicoBoard's sound sensor?

1. There is no alternative block.
2. The play sound block.
3. The loudness block.
4. The microphone block.

Q2. Why would you choose to use Scratch 1.4?

1. You want to use Scratch on the Raspberry Pi.
2. You want to use the source code.
3. Your current web browser does not support Flash.
4. All of the above.

Q3. What do the analog ports on the PicoBoard measure?

1. Sound.
2. Resistance.
3. Temperature.
4. Weather.

Summary

The PicoBoard makes Scratch programming tangible. We can hear the sounds we collect or feel the temperature we record through the analog ports. Scratch allows us to interpret those environmental stimuli through our projects whether we create a goofy talking head or more seriously chart measured data as part of an experiment.

The strength of the PicoBoard is that it gives us a new context to apply to our Scratch projects. We still use the same programming concepts, but the perspective of the information we have changes to things we can touch.

That's it! You have all the tools you need to turn your imagination and the imagination of your children into your very own mad scientists' laboratory.

Happy Scratching!

B
Pop Quiz Answers

Chapter 2, A Quick Start Guide to Scratch

Pop quiz – getting started with scratch

Q1	4
Q2	2
Q3	3
Q4	1
Q5	2

Chapter 3, Creating an Animated Birthday Card

Pop quiz – reviewing the chapter

Q1	4
Q2	3
Q3	4
Q4	1
Q5	3
Q6	1

Chapter 4, Creating a Scratch Story Book

Pop quiz – reviewing the chapter

Q1	2
Q2	1
Q3	4
Q4	3

Chapter 5, Creating a Multimedia Slideshow

Pop quiz – reviewing the chapter

Q1	2
Q2	2
Q3	2
Q4	3
Q5	4

Chapter 6, Making an Arcade Game – Breakout (Part I)

Pop quiz – reviewing the chapter

Q1	4
Q2	2
Q3	1
Q4	2
Q5	3

Chapter 9, Turning Geometric Patterns into Art Using the Pen Tool

Pop quiz – getting into shape

Q1	4
Q2	3
Q3	3

Appendix A, Connecting a PicoBoard to Scratch 1.4

Pop quiz – connecting to the real world

Q1	3
Q2	4
Q3	2

Index

U

Undelete option
  used, for undoing deletion 37
user-defined shapes
  drawing, sliders used 221-224
user instructions
  providing 130, 131

V

vector editing tools
  Color a shape 56
  Duplicate 56
  Ellipse 56
  Line 56
  Pencil 55
  Rectangle 56
  Reshape 55
  Select 55
vector images
  drawing 53, 54
  or bitmap images, choosing 53
  size, changing 54
video sensing feature
  about 46
video-sensing project
  reviewing 44, 45

W

wait () secs block 69
wait until () block
  about 157
webcam images
  animating, by sound detection 251-253
when backdrop switches to () block 117
when flag clicked block
  used, for hiding all sprites 62-64
when I receive (fortune) block 202
when I start as a clone block
  about 150
  used, for breaking bricks 148
whirl effect 71
word list
  building, text scanned for 211-213

X

x position block 137

Thank you for buying
Scratch 2.0 Beginner's Guide *Second Edition*

About Packt Publishing

Packt, pronounced 'packed', published its first book "Mastering phpMyAdmin for Effective MySQL Management" in April 2004 and subsequently continued to specialize in publishing highly focused books on specific technologies and solutions.

Our books and publications share the experiences of your fellow IT professionals in adapting and customizing today's systems, applications, and frameworks. Our solution-based books give you the knowledge and power to customize the software and technologies you're using to get the job done. Packt books are more specific and less general than the IT books you have seen in the past. Our unique business model allows us to bring you more focused information, giving you more of what you need to know, and less of what you don't.

Packt is a modern, yet unique publishing company, which focuses on producing quality, cutting-edge books for communities of developers, administrators, and newbies alike. For more information, please visit our website: www.PacktPub.com.

Writing for Packt

We welcome all inquiries from people who are interested in authoring. Book proposals should be sent to author@packtpub.com. If your book idea is still at an early stage and you would like to discuss it first before writing a formal book proposal, contact us; one of our commissioning editors will get in touch with you.

We're not just looking for published authors; if you have strong technical skills but no writing experience, our experienced editors can help you develop a writing career, or simply get some additional reward for your expertise.

Scratch Cookbook

ISBN: 978-1-84951-842-0   Paperback:262 pages

A quick and easy guide for building Scratch programs
intended for further learning through projects,
such as interactive animations and games

1. Get started using Scratch, or take your programs
    to a new level using simple, easy-to-read recipes.

2. Learn techniques for animating stories.

3. Create fun and engaging games.

Scratch 2.0 Game Development Hotshot

ISBN: 978-1-84969-756-9   Paperback: 330 pages

10 engaging projects that will teach you how
to build exciting games with the easy-to-use
Scratch 2.0 environment

1. Discover how to make the most of the
    new Scratch 2.0 interface.

2. Understand how video games work
    under the hood.

3. Make your projects come to life, using
    practical programming principles.

4. Learn how to plan and build your own
    interactive projects.

Please check **www.PacktPub.com** for information on our titles

GameSalad Beginner's Guide

ISBN: 978-1-84969-220-5   Paperback:308 pages

A fun, quick, step-by-step guide to creating games with levels, physics, sound, and numerous enemies using GameSalad

1. Learn to build three games; Ball Drop, Space Defender, and Metal Mech with GameSalad.

2. Complete these games with sound effects, use of physics, gravity, and collisions.

3. Learn tips and tricks to make a game popular straight from the author's own experience.

Unity Android Game Development by Example Beginner's Guide

ISBN: 978-1-84969-201-4   Paperback: 320 pages

Learn how to create exciting games using Unity 3D for Android with the help of hands-on examples

1. Enter the increasingly popular mobile market and create games using Unity 3D and Android.

2. Learn optimization techniques for efficient mobile games.

3. Clear, step-by-step instructions for creating a complete mobile game experience.

Please check **www.PacktPub.com** for information on our titles